The Beauty of Broken Things

Melissa Sharman

HAWKEYE

PUBLISHING

First published in Australia in 2026 by Hawkeye Publishing.

Cover Design by Skye Martin

This book is based on real events. To protect the privacy of people included in this book, some names have been changed.

A catalogue record of this book is available from the National Library of Australia.

ISBN 9781923105676

Proudly printed in Australia.

www.hawkeyebooks.com.au

I write from memory, from muscle and marrow, from a chest that still aches when it remembers. This is not a legal document. This is not the final authority. This is my story, shaped by what I recall, what I feel, and what my heart insists on naming. If you seek absolute truth, you may consult court files, police reports, or news archives. What I offer instead is the truth of experience – the tremor of a hand, the hollow of a room, the echo of voices that linger long after they have gone.

Some names have been changed to protect. Some characters are composites; others are shadows drawn from many. This is not to diminish accountability, but to safeguard the privacy of those who help illuminate what it feels like to live inside these events – navigating the spaces between fear, grief, and survival. The story belongs to me. It is not theirs.

I tell it imperfectly. Some memories have fractured, others sharpened, and some refuse to settle into a linear timeline. I have leaned on the recollections of others who witnessed what I could not face alone. Where dialogue faltered in memory, I reconstructed it, guided by intuition and emotional truth. I have left out what I cannot bear and changed what would cause harm.

I am telling the truth as I know it – not absolute, not complete, but mine. I am a survivor, not a possession, not a cautionary tale, not a statistic. I am many things – some named, some unnamed. I am the child of my history, the author of my present, and the keeper of my future. What follows is offered with care, honesty, and the hope that in reading it, you may find resonance, recognition, or release.

This is my story. This is my truth. It is imperfect, incomplete, and yet, entirely mine.

Melissa Sharman

For Mal, my steadfast anchor.

'Out of suffering have emerged the strongest souls; the most
massive characters are seared with scars. It is our scars, our
imperfections, that render us human, that imbue us with empathy
and compassion, that connect us to one
another in our shared humanity.'
– Khalil Gibran

Prologue

'It's over. Let me go.'

Seated on a charcoal-grey lounge in a marriage counsellor's office, I vacantly ran my fingertips across the textured fabric. Examining the room, I noticed framed photos on the desk, pictures of children beside a coffee mug reading 'Best Dad Ever.' The man before us had kind eyes and a solid presence; his name badge read 'Tony'. His voice steered us gently through a perfect storm.

His gaze passed between us; our chairs parted at a noticeable distance. His words were conciliatory, setting the rules of engagement for the session. Not wanting to be there, I avoided eye contact, my body unyielding. I felt betrayed, empty, and broken. The man I had vowed to love sat beside me, a stranger I no longer recognised.

Tony spoke to my husband, who began to explain our marital issues. Lucas's tone was meek; his voice shook, full of regret. 'I've done stupid things. But I love my family and want to make this marriage work.'

His words floated weightlessly, eliciting no empathy. I was void, the room hollow; the wind deflated from our sails, and we drifted in a vast ocean of hurt.

'I love you. Give me a chance to make this right.' He met my gaze, his eyes frantic. Sadness and anger ignited simultaneously with familiar promises – platitudes I'd heard before, my patience exhausted. The counsellor turned his attention to me. 'Do you want to work on your marriage?'

Both men looked at me intently, awaiting my answer.

During an imperceptible pause, I thought about the cost of answering fully and weighed it against the cost of silence. I finally replied, my voice measured, 'You're the fourth counsellor we've been to. We had the same conversations, and he's made the same promises. I don't believe them anymore. I'm not leaving because I don't love him. This is not the life I want for any of us. I want a divorce.'

Voices were muted and dull as waves of emotion pounded an already injured ship. Conceding the hurt entangled in my burnt-out eyes and closed body language, Tony nodded, swallowing but saying nothing. Finally, he released a deep breath. 'Thank you for coming in. If you ever need to talk, you're welcome to come back. You're free to go.'

He pushed forward in his office chair. Lucas sat silently, staring at the floor, his eyes wailing like a caged animal. His expression of sorrow was a punch to the senses. Despite my choice, I grieved the hurt I caused the man I loved. The dull ache sent ripples through me as I left the office, pulling the heavy glass door closed behind me and making my way to the car park.

I trembled as I unlocked the car and slumped into the front seat, my shaking hands gripping the steering wheel. Tears stung my eyes, hot, red, and swollen, and I ran my fingers through the tangled hair clinging to my cheeks. I wiped my eyes, mascara streaking the back of my hand. Looking into the rear-view mirror,

I stared deeply into my reflection. I'd become everything I despised: weak, brittle, broken. I didn't like what I saw, my eyes hollow, my skin pale.

I could not forget my daughters' looks of confusion and distress as they whimpered on the lounge room floor. The walls of our home held family photographs; vacation snapshots taken on happier days. The highlight reel of a vibrant, auspicious life was never what it seemed. Our secrets were jagged rocks under a high tide, ready to tear holes in an old flimsy boat.

I drove home wondering how I would ever feel okay again. Dark and hopeless, teetering on the edge of a bottomless chasm of despair, there were also glimmers of hope. Something had shifted, maybe slightly, but perceptibly. I had to be brave enough to break my own heart, even when it threatened to dismantle life piece by piece.

And here begins the story. An unrelenting wildfire had burned through my life and taken everything, devouring the arid landscape in its wake. A pain radiated, I had been stripped bare, broken down and pared back to the brittle bones. Yet, from the ashes, the devastation brought regrowth, little shoots of life beckoned from a blackened wasteland, bringing a new beginning.

It crept through me like a seedling, spreading its roots beneath the soil. A renewed sense of purpose was taking shape. Fire causes both damage and destruction and triumph and transformation. It's possible for two opposing things to be simultaneously true at once. A counsellor once told me to 'wish for more pain' – because it's how we as humans change. The ache and discomfort cause us to do things differently; it forces our hand.

I say this not to compare to or detract from anybody else's truth. I'm simply speaking my own. One person's suffering does not invalidate, diminish, or overshadow another's. Nor does their success. I had to move into – and through – the darkness to find the beauty.

So, I write this for anyone needing to hear it, for anyone who has been broken. For anyone wondering how the hell they got there. May some small part of my story resonate at some level with yours. There is hope beyond your pain, a purpose beyond your brokenness. There is beauty within the wreckage, in recreation and transformation. I didn't realise it then, but I'd just taken the first steps toward the rest of my life.

1

When I was fifteen, a friend and I snuck out to a party under the cover of darkness. We arrived to find it in full swing, music pulsing and a sea of bodies moving in unison like breaking waves. Those who entered the torrent, drinks in hand, were swallowed whole, devoured by the current of intoxicated human bodies. Strobe lights threw orbs in luminescent bursts onto the crowd of silhouetted dancers. Teens drank straight from bottles and smoked weed and cigarettes in dark corners.

Girls bared their tawny, tanned skin, their tiny skirts showing off their long legs. They hung off the shoulders of boys in baggy, low-hanging pants before disappearing into the shadows of the yard, only the orange glow of their cigarette lights visible. Clusters of people were seated in circles on camping chairs and rustic wooden crates. Discarded beer cans were dispersed across the rocky driveway, a haze of blue smoke wafted out of the back shed, the pulsing bass drawing me in.

In the midst of strangers, I was anonymous, uninhibited, and unrestrained. I envied the girls who felt comfortable enough to be who they were, how easily they breathed. Downing shots of rum, I felt alive; my senses heightened and dulled simultaneously.

We lay on a picnic blanket in the early hours behind an old Queenslander, under a macadamia nut tree and camellia plants with their heavy white flowers, the air thick with the scent of soil and dawn. Around us, bodies slept off the night before, soft breaths rising like mist. For a brief moment, wrapped in someone else's discarded jacket, I imagined a version of myself who felt whole, untouched, free. That version flickered like a candle in the wind – but she was there. The horizon glowed a faint pastel orange and pink, awaiting sunrise. I tried to pinpoint the exact moment daylight was switched on. The long night had contours worn smooth by sea, diversion from my saw-toothed anger. Again and again, my anger simmered beneath the surface before bubbling over.

Something deep inside, already hanging by a thread, had finally broken. I'd seen the world as a place of good. Raised in a religious family, that part of my identity was intertwined; primal, integral. It ran deeper than memory and habit and transcended thought. Woven into every fibre of my being, my faith in God had been my north star, a guiding light. That truth now felt shaky.

I rebelled with bottles of spirits, cool colours and angular lines a kaleidoscope blurring my periphery. I didn't know if I still believed in God. I certainly didn't believe in me.

Grief, anger, self-loathing – as ancient as bone. My memories refused to hold steady, surfacing and vanishing in shards of light, leaving me raw and restless. Yet the fire inside would not die; it smouldered the way embers cling to heat long after the blaze is over. And the reason for my anger? It was the only truth left standing. A few weeks prior to the party, a church program led me to a volunteer group with a green-eyed man. Still haunted by flashbacks of his mouth on mine, the stubble of his face, and the weight of his body, I could feel his hands pulling at my clothes. It evoked the sharp scent of his cologne and the way he looked at me. No man had ever looked at me like this, and I had not recognised it.

Arriving to collect me in his work van, he stood by the driver's door in heavy, navy overalls, splashed with multicoloured smears. His fingernails were short and dirty, knuckles dry and marked in peeling patches of white paint. He was dressed differently from the man I saw on Sundays.

He drove down narrow roads bordered by rows of sugarcane, the towering stalks swaying gently. Sunlight filtered through the dense canopy, casting dappled shadows on the bitumen ahead. Pulling into a driveway, he halted outside a large brick home. He smiled. 'Come on in. I won't be long. I need to change.'

Sauntering up the driveway, his keys jangled as he unlocked the front door and stepped inside, holding it open behind him. Anxiety set fire to my senses, spooked instincts battling with the learned importance of being polite. I hesitantly followed. The room was ordinary with worn furniture and washing draped over a chair. A stack of men's magazines was spread across the coffee table. He brushed past me, collecting a shirt and moving towards the bathroom, closing the door behind him.

I leaned against a desk by the door while he showered. Flicking through a catalogue and checking my watch impatiently, I willed him to hurry. As though he'd read my mind, the pipes shuttered and the sound of flowing water ceased. Moments later, the bathroom door opened, steam escaping into the room. The bitter aroma of men's cologne hit my nostrils, intense and sharp. I wrinkled my nose.

Standing by the bathroom door, a thick canary-yellow towel hung around his waist. Droplets of water beaded on his bare, sun-weathered chest and tattooed arms. He seemed to be searching for something before leaning over my body, pressing me against the desk. I froze. Grasping the nape of my neck with his hands, he pulled me in.

I felt his lips on mine, my shirt being pulled up, his hands on my breasts.

Oh shit.

I jerked my shoulders, recoiling. My stomach dropped, hands trembling.

'No,' was all I could get out. He ignored the rebuff, pushing closer, determined. My heart pounded, panic hyping my pulse.

His weight pinned me against the desk. My breath caught in my throat as I twisted under him, trying to wrench free. His grip tightened at the back of my neck and for a moment I felt trapped-small, overpowered, the air thick with the sudden realisation of what might happen next. Fear surged through me, hot and electric, drowning out everything except the need to get away.

I pushed my knees hard into his upper thighs, forcing him to stumble momentarily. As he dropped his towel, I seized the opportunity, sliding across the desk and out the door.

He cursed, bending to pick it up, his naked body exposed. The screen door jolted as I tumbled onto the concrete, loose gravel grazing my skin. Struggling to my feet, I sprinted down the driveway, along the roadside, and sought cover behind a decaying stump.

I was stymied, suspended in time, afraid to tell my parents what had happened; they would blame me. I called a friend on my old

Nokia phone, and he soon came to find me, dropping me off at a youth centre shack in a historic sugarcane town. I was grateful.

The green-eyed man soon arrived but not a word was exchanged. His eyes played cat and mouse as I evaded the glower demanding silence. Making myself small, I felt myself curl inwards, trying to stay out of sight. My mother collected me a few hours later, with no questions about why plans had changed. I sat silent as she listened to church music on the car stereo.

As I lay in bed, stormy weather resounded outside my window, droplets drumming on the tin roof of our A-frame home like impatient fingertips. Water raced through the downpipes, a chorus swelling into a restless symphony as emotion inundated me. I questioned how the night had gone so wrong.

The sound felt ancient, like something my bones had always known. I remember wondering if maybe, somewhere far away, someone else was listening to the same storm. I liked the idea of not being entirely alone in it. That thought – tiny and soft – became something I carried forward, like a pebble tucked into my pocket, grounding me in its quiet weight. I'd put godly relationships on a pedestal. A perfect love story I believed was promised to the obedient, the steadfast. My idealistic worldview had been irreparably damaged. But like many things kept hidden, it was soon brought into the light.

I told a friend, she told another. The pastor heard about it and called me to his office to see him, listening and promising he would take care of it, before he swept it under the rug. I didn't understand the nuances of religious politics back then, and a fifteen-year-old girl and an incident with a philandering man wasn't a righteous testament to God's institution. It was a red wine stain on an ashen rug, and it was quickly removed from sight. This was fine with me. I felt humiliated and wanted it all to go away.

Conversations in quiet corners continued for months, and the green-eyed man continued to attend church each Sunday, his arm around his fiancée, his expression smug. Her eyes fixed on me with disdain as their wedding day neared. To her, I was a harlot – a home wrecker. Soon after, I stopped attending church.

It punched at my self-esteem and my faith. I didn't know it then, but the green-eyed man had come to the church to escape a dark past. Released on parole into a sexual offender treatment program for crimes against children, the church thought they could cure him from his dark illness. They believed in redemption and second chances, in playing saviour. If he attended church, found a wife, and followed their rules, he could reintegrate back into civilised society as a good Christian man.

Five years later, he took a thirteen-year-old boy in a red t-shirt from a Sunshine Coast bus stop.

The abduction and murder of Daniel Morcombe made headlines across the country, and photos of the green-eyed-man – Brett Peter Cowan – were splashed across every bulletin.

Years later, Cowan was sentenced to life in prison, and I was sentenced to a life of 'what-ifs'. In retrospect, I realised the structure of faith built around me was flimsy and fabricated. I ran from religion and all its lines and fences, created to protect tradition and institutions, a skin we must fit, a flock we must follow. I would rather burn than be a hypocrite.

Soon after, was that party, where booze drowned thought, memories, and disappointment. Those older kids were the epitome of cool, and I was drawn to them. I wanted their clothes, attitudes, toys, lives, and attention. They had it together and weren't afraid of anything or anyone. Unlike me – since the night of my sexual assault by the older green-eyed man, the man I was led to believe I could trust because of his ties to our church – my pain was buried in the church's quiet corners, hidden where no light could reach. I was left with nothing but the burden of my own immaturity: too young to know how to hold it, too unformed to even understand what I was trying to absorb, let alone how to survive it.

I remember reading that anger is a secondary emotion, the primary emotion is one of pain. Anger is hurt's bodyguard. In the months following, the anger withdrew, throwing down its sword, with sadness filling the pothole it once occupied. I found ways to dull the ache, struggling to contain my sadness and anxiety. I scratched my skin until I tore myself open, trying to make my suffering visible. At the time, I didn't have adequate language for my pain, so I used the body, the one thing that always told the truth. There was strange comfort in the burn, validation that I was still here, still capable of feeling something. That mattered, even if I couldn't admit it then.

I lost my appetite. Things holding pleasure or joy slipped away, inhabiting a state of anhedonia. Gazing out the window and into the paling sky, life's bright colours dissolved, leaving mottled grey. Perpetually numb, I retreated.

My teachers didn't know what to do with me. I was a broken window, a voided space, an erratic animal they didn't want to spook. So, they tiptoed around me, mostly leaving me alone. They gave me wide eyes and wider hall passes. One even handed me a wellbeing journal that smelled like lavender oil and denial. I appreciated the gesture. Mostly, I doodled skulls and wrote poetry in the margins. It was something.

My parents couldn't handle me either; we were a family that didn't trade in emotions. They kept their distance while I kept my secrets. Shutting my family out, I withdrew from friends. I spiralled into sadness, keeping distance between myself and anyone who might want to save my ravaged soul. I realised both had their demons.

Insurgence and obedience were two different types of cages. Both lived in reaction to someone else's way of being. I was ablaze with bitterness, self-loathing, and anger. Finally, I hit rock bottom.

The moment was evident to me as I lay in a hospital paediatric ward, my teenage frame incongruous in a place etched with cartoon animals. The room was dark, with a curtain pulled around the bed. I was unsure whether it was to protect me from the others in the room or them from me. The night was quiet, only the chirping and beeping of medical monitors and the sporadic cries of small children breaking the silence. Having shut everyone out, I had never felt so alone. As a child, I'd been spirited, headstrong. That lively part of me had become muted. I was just floating, discarded driftwood washed up by the tide.

Earlier, my anxiety had hit a peak. Pain tablets, promising numbness, tranquillity, and solitude, called to me from my dresser drawer. Taken to the hospital after overdosing on pills, I wanted to feel less of everything – less sadness, less exhaustion, and less angst. This choice didn't bring the result I'd hoped for.

It brought me a social worker named Julie and twelve months of therapy. I wasn't the first pissed-off, defiant, angst-ridden teen to cross her path. When I first noticed her sitting beside my hospital bed, she looked at me with warmth and empathy.

'Go away. I don't want to talk to you,' I spat, irritated at her unwelcome intrusion. My teenage obstinacy was formidable; I had no intentions of spilling my pain to a stranger. Thankfully, she disregarded my dismissals, slowly chipping away at the walls I'd built to keep her and everyone else out. Soon, she broke them down, gaining my trust.

Julie had honey-blonde curls framing her pretty face, her fair skin dusted with light freckles. I grew to like her. Her green cat-like eyes twinkled when she talked. Her stubbornness matched mine, and over the coming months, with her gentle prodding and much self-work, the sadness and anger slowly dissipated.

As the dark shadow over my life steadily lifted, I saw life in colour again. I let people in. The change meant new friendships began to flourish. During this time, I learned about myself and the world I inhabited. I always felt oddly out of place in my family without understanding why. My childhood held patchy memories bleeding into one another.

The photographs of my sister and me with pigtails were a single snapshot, a lone frame lost on the cutting room floor, devoid of narrative. Memory can be a fickle creature, a storytelling beast. From dusty albums and stories on the pages, my mind put them together like an old movie flowing in a dream sequence. It seeks to give them chronology, to create a better narrative than the one I remember. I find pieces of unmapped recollections and self-truths, deciphering them carefully. I can't remember many insignificant details, the conversations, playing games, or the everyday routines. Other information I'll never forget: the places we went, faces and names and the intricate details of events, the sounds, the smells, and, most importantly, how they made me feel.

Many memories are jagged. My nanna gave me a porcelain doll with alabaster skin and red lips. She wore a scarlet suit with a matching cap, and I named her Lizzie. I cradled her with the care of a baby bird. She reminded me that delicate things could be beautiful too — fragile, yes, but not worthless. She quickly became one of my favourite things.

One day, my father, enraged, smashed her feet with a rod. He must have felt guilty after, because he tried to repair the damage he had caused, clumsily sewing her boots back onto her feet with uneven, mismatched stitches. Lizzie had been perfect before she became a symbol of irreparable damage.

Years later, I would remember that doll when trying to explain myself to therapists — how some damage isn't visible, how sometimes the stitching shows.

In truth, Lizzie was only a mirror — her fractured porcelain reflecting the quiet truth that nothing in our world was beyond breaking. A glass cabinet, bedroom doors, our little bodies — all became casualties of a rage that even he seemed powerless to control. Through the looking glass of therapy, I now see that my parents came from very different backgrounds. My father was born into poverty, with a violent, abusive father and a passive but comforting 'saviour' mother. His authoritarian father ruled with an iron fist, and children were seen but not heard. Generational paradigms are complex circuits to break.

A lone acorn fell from a towering oak and produced another tall oak, duplicated but decades apart. My father was a solitary figure we both revered and feared, flesh and blood, both familiar and foreign to us simultaneously. He was the first domino in a line, laid and set. My relationship with my dad set the standard for other men who walked into my life behind him.

My mother was born into a wealthy but dysfunctional family where childhood was confusing, inhospitable, and often unsafe. Tormented and scapegoated by a narcissistic mother and subjected to the highest standards of a father whose approval she could only wish to gain. Together, my parents tried their best to form a functional family from the rubble of two dysfunctional childhoods. When they found their faith in God, my parents adopted a version of religion safest for them to raise a family: black and white. Right and wrong as they understood it. It was a set of standards or a version of theology they abided by, which they felt protected them. For them, anything uncomfortable or unfamiliar was wrong, and they would shut it out. Muslims, gay people, immigrants: these were all topics treated much like other scary things. Avoid, don't discuss it, don't make eye contact, or engage.

Fear causes people to act irrationally. They had childhoods they couldn't control, so as adults, they feared anything upsetting their comfort and disturbing their equilibrium. Those lessons were introduced early. My life was narrated by others. What was righteous and sinful, the patterns and orders of life, and my relationships with others were drawn along biblical doctrine.

What we believed was defined by men – our church pastor, my father, and other figures of regarded righteousness. Whether television evangelists or community leaders, their voices were all-consuming. Any free thinking was swallowed by a stronger current of tradition and religious dogma, and our home life existed within these confines.

My father had two distinct sides. In the outside world, he had a larger-than-life personality. Outgoing and friendly, he spent time with his mates and in the community at cricket, card nights, and fundraising events. He was a doer, a leader. For a while, I felt envious of the people who surrounded him, those who secured his interest when I had failed to. At home, time spent with us was often loaded. He was the breadwinner who worked hard, but when we saw him, he retreated to the lounge and the glow of the television, vacant and distant and not to be bothered.

My father's way of showing love was with food. His happy moments were when our family sat together around a meal. It was his currency, and because of his upbringing, being a provider was fundamental to him. Mostly, though, he watched us grow up from behind a one-way mirror. I wondered if parenting was foreign to him, a skin that never quite fit.

My mother managed part-time jobs with parenting and domestic responsibilities. She was a mellow contrast to my father's jagged edges, offering structure and stability to our lives. My mother was an intelligent woman who underestimated her worth. She was a martyr to everyone else's needs, sacrificing herself. She kept us busy playing and learning and taught us to ride bikes, bake, and make things. She introduced us to music and songs. She met our physical needs the best she knew how. Raised in a family that didn't show love or emotion, she didn't have these tools to pass on to the next generation. I remember making crafts and collecting ladybirds in jars in our backyard. The rare quiet moments when my mother hugged me and told me loving things, made me fly.

Overall, my parents were a mystery to me, both familiar and elusive. My nanna told me stories about my father growing up and how he met my mother. I discovered photographs of my parents in a brown vinyl album in her sewing cupboard. My mother was a pale, mousey young girl attached to my father, her face expressionless, head down. Insecure, dependent, almost fusing into the surrounding scenery. In the photograph, my father leaned over her, his elbow on her shoulder. His stance was cocky with a youthful swagger, and his thick hair swept over his face. I recognised those hazel eyes and the confidence that bled into youthful arrogance. They seemed an odd pairing even back then. Perhaps they found something in each other, missing in themselves. I had no idea when the strangers in those photographs became the people I knew as my parents.

Their three children, my younger siblings – sister Elle, my brother Robbie – and I, were the willow tree, bending in the wind, flexible and malleable so as not to break. We moved with life; we adapted and grew. After I was born, Elle was born twenty-one months later, and Robbie followed three years after her.

We learned the importance of service. Beyond the hardships and challenges, there was some good. But that's nostalgia. The injurious memories sifted out to leave the good.

For the longest time, we understood little beyond the fences they put up to guide us, to create and shape our reality and worldview. My mother encouraged reading; she taught me how to be curious. My father taught me men were something to fear. An unknown quantity in a mathematical equation, an enigma.

From when I was young, I had a stubborn need to be independent. I've never been afraid to speak up about things I'm passionate about, even if everyone else in the room disagrees. I love nothing more than an interesting conversation.

During the third grade, I discovered books, with the library becoming a sanctuary for me as I read anything and everything – novels, essays, magazines, and newspapers. Introduced to ideas and issues, particularly on social justice, travel, literature, and culture, subtly helped shape my worldview without me even recognising it. The new ideas collided with my learned beliefs, but the conflict and divergence were a composition that was thought-provoking, coexisting but not competing, gradually picking undone former perspectives.

In the years preceding the dawn of the new millennium, when Yahoo chat was innovative and the virtual meeting place on dial-up internet, the mere prospect of serendipitous encounters with the expanse of humanity across the digital ether stirred within me a profound sense of excitement. Their stories and these fleeting connections held such possibility to someone who didn't feel much of a connection to anything. They were a welcome distraction from my insecurity, the exchange of colloquial lyrics entwined and arranged into a symphony of keystrokes, line by line, synchronised and looping into a virtual world that hummed into a song. Life held endless possibilities behind the fences. I wanted to gallop. I wanted to explore and to fly. It is all part of the story.

2

I was sixteen when I met THE ONE. The great Romeo and Juliet, ride-or-die, tragic love story of my life. The story had all the elements of an infamous tale of romance. We lived oceans apart, and initially, he belonged to someone else. After nights of conversation passed quickly in time and between souls, I soon found my resistance to his charms faltering, his words reaching me. Finding a place long abandoned, they left my teenage heart smitten.

He had flown to Australia to visit a friend. My father took an instant dislike to the young, sandy-haired Texan boy with his cocky American confidence, swagger, and loud, outspoken opinions, and was determined to drive us apart. With my teenage insolence and little other love to grip onto, it made me want him more. We had big dreams and no means and before long, conversations turned from minutes into hours as we talked into the night. Other barriers fell away, and I was head-over-heels in young love. My parents kicked me out of the house, their alternative to facing a conversation with their teenage daughter about love and growing up.

I went to live in a university dormitory on campus which inevitably offered both advantages and disadvantages to a teenage girl. It offered newfound independence and a sense of freedom, but also the responsibility of surviving on a measly student payment and the proceeds of a low-paying after-school job. I attended high school but lived with older students who were navigating their own freedom, cramming for exams, sleeping through the days, and partying the nights away. Any real-world lessons my conservative upbringing had deprived me of, I caught up on fast.

My housemates gave me a fake ID and a crash course on student party life. I arrived at school after four hours' sleep with mascara-smudged eyes and a bright green nightclub stamp blurred across my wrist. I remember those nights as long. I'd always been a night owl, usually going to bed later, but still my circadian rhythms were at odds with the cadence of university life, which was built around partying students. Somehow, I juggled all of it. I tried to keep busy, because in the moments I paused, reality hit. I was lonely and felt abandoned by my family, the people who were supposed to love me the most.

At night, my beau and I spoke about the future, our pasts, and all the half-formed things we dreamed into being. At sixteen, he spoke like someone who already knew his way in the world, and I clung to that certainty like a lifeboat. Being pushed from home had cast me adrift, and a person can only tread water so long before they go under. He gave my restlessness a place to land; he threw me a lifeline. His voice, steady through the phone line, felt like warm light under a door I hadn't yet opened. I didn't know then that this kind of love could both save and sink you. But for a time, it gave me something to swim toward.

He'd finished school early, passed his GED, had a driver's licence, and a good job.

Still in his youth, the hours he spent working out at the gym gave him a man's physique, stark overcompensation for the years as a chubby child tormented by his peers. He wore his heart on his sleeve, and his voice at the end of the line was the warmest security blanket. A safe place. An anchor in a stormy sea.

We talked about things that mattered, things I was hungry to discuss with someone. Anyone. His words painted vibrant colours and described shapes of things I'd never seen or felt before. A love and acceptance I only dreamed of. I collected his time and attention like shiny trinkets, adding these to a small but bright collection, tangible proof I was worthy of being loved and everything would be okay.

He told me about his town, family, and all his ghosts and secrets. He lived through abuse from his father and never quite felt enough. With much in common, there were many things I didn't need to explain. He cared, reaching me where others had tried and failed. His body became an idea I dragged into bed with me at night. An escape from life, he was home, albeit one I'd never lived in. I wasn't alone anymore.

I wanted to be anywhere but that university dorm. I took up space, breathed borrowed oxygen, just existing – a girl in waiting, hoping to transcend into a life with shape and meaning. I didn't know it then, but survival itself was a kind of sacred act. In those dull, grey days, I was quietly storing strength, brick by brick. I left school and began working long hours at two jobs to save for a plane ticket, every dollar saved in a yellow envelope. Living on bread and instant noodles, the promise of a better life was the fuel powering me through hunger and fatigue. At seventeen, I boarded a flight to the United States with nothing but a backpack, quiet hope, and the kind of belief only the very young or very broken can carry. As the plane rose above the clouds, I watched my past shrink beneath me – a country I'd always lived in, but not one that held any kind of home. I didn't know where I would land, not truly. But some part of me already understood that even if this wasn't the place I was meant to stay, it was a place I could survive. And that, in itself, was something.

When my plane landed at a regional airport, a group gathered behind a fence, I searched from the windows, looking for his face. On a large metal aviation hangar, read a sign 'Welcome to Waco, Texas.' Setting foot on the dusty tarmac was a surreal experience.

More handsome than I remembered, he stood in the arrivals area in a black t-shirt, sneakers, and blue jeans, holding a bouquet of freshly cut bluebonnets. I met his gentle eyes, seeing a look of wonder, and relief washed over me. When he pulled me into his arms, I felt his heart beating through his shirt. Collecting up my bags from the carousel and helping me into his burgundy Chevy, we drove from the airport, merging onto a freeway. Dilapidated industrial sheds, boarded-up warehouses, and underpasses marked with graffiti lined the roads, and billboards along the shoulder advertised teeth whitening, cell phone plans, and fast-food outlets. Leaving the freeway, there were rows of convenience stores, gas stations, and Baptist churches on every second corner.

The excitement of the new scenery heightened my senses as I took in this new place. After a few days hiding away in a downtown motel, he finally introduced me to his mother.

Charlene was a curvy, big-haired woman with heavy make-up and a thick Southern drawl. Single for a long time, she was the family matriarch who called all the shots despite having two fully grown sons. Raised to revere their mama, ours was a relationship of three. The intrusion was initially subtle, passing comments before helpful suggestions took on a more forceful tone. A girl seeking the approval of a new mother-in-law will let many things pass without issue.

They decided the clothing I had was unsuitable, telling me men would look at me, and I wasn't for their eyes. It was because he loved me, he said. She took me shopping for a new wardrobe. It reflected my new, 'more mature' look: no tops that showed bust line and skirts that hung below the knees. Office apparel or my Sunday best were the clothing that emulated his mother's style but complying avoided arguments.

He's protective because he loves me, I told myself.

Things changed from carefree to serious at a rapid rate.

'Y'all should go and get married,' his mother declared in her Southern drawl. I could tell by her tone it was not a suggestion. In the days following, I overheard phone calls between Charlene and my parents.

'They can't live in sin. They need to be wed,' she pressed, requesting they sign marriage papers for their underage daughter. As stubborn as my father was, I suspected he was no match for her bull-headed persistence. I knew my parents had relented because her mood improved, and the calls stopped. She informed us I could stay in the USA to get married and apply for a green card. So, she organised a wedding. In three hours, she bought a cake and flowers. I wore a formal dress I had brought along from home. Black satin. The kind worn to evening affairs or funerals, not weddings.

The cake was a vanilla sponge from the supermarket, topped with white imitation frosting. I smiled in photos, too dazed to speak, clutching my bouquet. Years later, I'd realise that wasn't a beginning – it was a mirror, reflecting everything I still needed to learn about love, agency, and myself. The wedding was worlds away from how I'd imagined it. His grandmother's new husband, a reverend, signed the papers a few days later in a Mexican restaurant after a trip to the local county courthouse. The honeymoon was at a mid-range hotel next door to a sizeable southern-style restaurant. Even then, it felt surreal, like someone else's story, a terrible midday movie.

When I left Australia, I gave little thought to what would happen beyond arriving at the airport or what 'happily ever after' might look like. Raised in the Disney generation, with fairytales and happy endings, our predictable love story seemed to write itself.

The reality of young love was far less romantic. I spent the first few months hidden away in a tiny apartment. He told me it was a dangerous neighbourhood, so I spent nine hours a day watching trashy daytime television talk shows. A bored and lonely housewife, I waited faithfully for my new husband to return home.

Later, we moved in with his mother, brother, and his brother's wife. We would go out for long drives, cuddle up on the couch with a movie, cook, pay bills, and imitate adults with their shit together. Life was monotonous, the shiny lustre of new love wearing off as life became repetitious. I began working in a department store and he had a job at a local pawnbroker shop.

Blindly optimistic, I scrambled to fill a deep void in my life and to find somewhere I belonged. My parents had cast me out, and that Texan town, as hard as I tried to love it, was unfamiliar and overwhelming. This is the conundrum of those who don't belong – there is a pull to reinvent ourselves unhindered by our history in a bright new city, to put our old selves away in a drawer. To expunge and purge it, to forge a new path and new identity, one in which we belong. Without the maturity to manage my happiness, I felt trapped in the expectations that my upbringing and religion had set for me. In the end, we were both unhappy in our relationship.

We first spoke about marriage in the early days of our relationship. It was the ultimate expression of validation, love, and acceptance. Raised in Christian homes, it was hard to tell whose was more dysfunctional. Our upbringing came with expectations, and we rationalised marriage as the 'right' way to be together. The health of our relationship was marred by a myriad of issues and the nineties purity culture still going strong in the new millennium. Young and naïve, we were too young to know what we wanted from our lives. In hindsight, there were missteps and red flags on both sides.

My independence was lost when we got married. I left friends and family and couldn't drive. With a moratorium on my time, making friends was intricate. I couldn't buy a soda without permission, couldn't leave without announcing where I was going. Freedom tasted in spoonfuls, rationed and fleeting, and I didn't know until it was gone how sacred it was. He wasn't controlling – not in ways that could be named – but every misstep sank into me, and guilt spread through me like ink in water. Love folded itself around me, a pattern of tethering that whispered, 'I care,' even as it bound me tighter than I knew. Later, I would learn to guard that freedom like fire, to measure love not by its grip, but by the spaces it left for me to breathe.

He did his best, but circumstances were a by-product of my choices.

I grew to resent him for all I'd given up. Maybe he felt the same. As tensions escalated, holes were punched in the drywall. His acoustic guitar busted open over a chair as his temper flared, splinters stuck like wooden teeth in the carpet. The lightness and air turned to crude oil. Expression hindered, speech was congealed, and growth stunted. My world spun on a different axis, wobbly and out of sync.

Not since childhood had I felt such a sense of trepidation, of skittishness. He never told me I should fear him, but the holes in the wall watched over me like a full moon illuminating our room. He didn't have to say a word. Passionate and emotional, he didn't lay a hand on me, but his moods were a perfect storm on the horizon, and I sheltered in place. I learned to read the sky like weather – to prepare, to shrink, to disappear before the first crack of thunder. It would take me years to unlearn that shrinking. But my body knew how to survive, even then. It never stopped trying to keep me safe.

In the narrative of a young Christian marriage, failure wasn't an option. But eventually, we did fail. There was no pivotal moment or single fight. No one saw it coming so soon. As quickly as we had come together, we fell apart. Days later, I boarded a flight home. He wouldn't look at me on the way to the airport, and I fought to hold it together.

As I returned home to Australia, life had moved on without me. I began studying, playing sports, a new job, and volunteering at schools with disadvantaged students, each a distraction from the feeling of overwhelming failure. I was the prodigal daughter coming home.

My parents must have known it would all end in disaster and waited for my homecoming with more than a hint of 'I told you so'. There were no meaningful conversations to let me unload my grief, no wiping of tears, pep talks, and no passing down of parental wisdom.

I was grieving and they pushed me to get over it and move on. I grieved in silence.

I joined a divorce support program at the local church. I can look back now and laugh about how it must have appeared for an eighteen-year-old girl to attend such a group. Disgrace sat heavy on my shoulders; it was more than I should have ever been allowed to bear alone. As a young woman, a newly minted adult, I didn't have the awareness, psychological support, or maturity to navigate this life tangle of trauma.

I carried the shame silently inside my body and mind. I remember the hollow feeling of losing my first love, slipping into a black abyss, and wanting it all back, as uncomfortable as it was. If I'd ever had any grace in company, I had lost it.

I felt like a broken bird after a long convalescence, feathers frayed, trying clumsily to relearn how to fly. But even broken wings remember the wind. And in time, I would too – not with grace, but with grit. Each awkward take-off was proof that I hadn't forgotten how to move toward the sky.

I sat alone in a park, shielding my tears from the world, blowing on dandelions as if they were prayers in disguise. The puffs scattered on the wind – tiny, weightless fragments of hope. I wished then to be whole again. It didn't come the way I expected, or when I expected it. But looking back now, I know this: healing was already happening in the quiet. I just didn't yet know how to recognise it.

What we want is seldom what we need. The bright-eyed teenager boarding the flight a year before was replaced by a tired, broken woman. Shattered porcelain, once a thing of beauty, hastily pieced back together, rough edges and uneven lines. I felt inherently flawed, believing my value lay in the validation of others, and struggled to feel peace within my body. Growing up with repetitive messaging around sex being dirty and virginity being the pinnacle of value and beauty, I had a lot to fear of my body. Feeling broken, used, and dirty, I wondered if anyone would ever want me.

I threw myself into work at a job in telecommunications and as a business representative, required to attend functions with important people, to show up, stand up straight and smile.

Holly, a beautiful doe-eyed colleague who had recently relocated from interstate, made the mandatory events bearable. Whisking me off towards the trays of canapés and champagne, she would flirt shamelessly with the agents who gave away expensive sample products, bagging us the latest flip phones and branded gift bags. She pulled me out to the nightclubs afterwards, her laughter a crazed riot drawing others in. Holly would throw her head back and wrinkle her nose, drinking champagne from the bottle, and I knew we would be in for a wild night. Returning hungover the next morning, we'd drink down a Red Bull and eat a bacon-and-egg burger before pulling ourselves together for the workday. I drank a lot of shitty coffee that year.

Our male colleagues were vultures, working in packs, preying on unsuspecting clients who left with expensive products in sales bags before they knew what had hit them. I played the game differently. I listened to clients, showed kindness and confidence, and if they had issues, I would do my best to help. I looked them in the eyes and showed them I cared. I followed the number one rule of working with people: don't be a dick.

I liked my job, and it gave me a reason to get up, go to work, function as a contributing member of society again. To belong somewhere, do something, and be someone, giving me a sense of routine and purpose. I needed symmetry and structure and to colour within the lines for a while.

3

While I was heartbroken and healing, I met Lucas. He was a simple, unpretentious boy fleeing a country town that suffocated him, looking for bright city lights and a better life. He had dropped out of school and had kids young. He was twenty-two, with a couple of children from a previous relationship, who lived with their mother. The idea of fraternising with a man with any responsibility for other small humans, seemed foolish. I felt too young for that kind of responsibility. Our conversations were playful and light.

Quietly spoken and easy to talk to, he'd made his fair share of mistakes and never judged mine. There was a quiet gravity to him, a softness beneath rough edges that pulled me in, even though I knew deep down he wasn't right for me. Sometimes, the heart recognises comfort, even when logic raises red flags – a survival instinct of its own.

His warmth slipped through my defences like a house cat weaving at my ankles, purring softly, carving tiny spaces of trust in the cold fortress I'd built. In those moments, I felt a fragile thread of connection – a quiet sign that maybe I could feel again. Understanding him was careful, almost imperceptible, work, like watching sediment settle in still water.

We met in person with friends at a bar. I hung back, guarded.

In his company, the ebbs and flows of life had begun moving again, though I still felt out of my depth. With vulnerability came fragility and I wasn't sure I would ever be ready for that again.

As darkness fell, we drove to the beach. Strings of lights arched overhead, tracing the Esplanade in soft illumination. Groups gathered around picnic tables, neon-lit restaurants and nightclubs, laughter spilling into the night. The beach itself was calm, the breeze gentle, the black sky sequined with stars. Playful, we kicked at powdery sand and let the saltwater lap at our toes. Feeling the chill of the waves and the ease of the moment, I let myself relax, letting the present settle quietly around me.

Watching Lucas from a comfortable distance, I sought the familiarity of our long phone conversations and found my heart softening. He was the sun, the light at the end of a long darkness. At first, he was so calm and quiet, I thought my curse of grief was broken.

I was falling for him.

I knew by the way he looked at me, he was already there. We stood close, but not too close, the air so thick, I was swimming in it.

Within days, he packed up his car and moved to be near me. For someone hungry for validation, it was flattering he believed I was worth the sacrifice, even when I wasn't ready to commit to a relationship. He stayed with my friends in a shared house, and my time there became more frequent. Disassembling my walls, brick by brick, I let down my guard.

He picked me up from work, red roses on the passenger seat. We took long drives on country roads, and he brought cups of freshly brewed tea as we watched movies at night. He revealed stories from his childhood; the arid landscape dotted with anguish.

With few friends, and messy past relationships, he narrated tales of woe of women who had been cruel and controlling. I felt protective of him, driven by a desire to shield and care for him.

Within months, we began living together. Our new apartment was airy, open, and a short walk from the beach. The crush of the surf echoed from the distance; the cool ocean breeze filled the curtains like sails.

The change in him was at first subtle, a slow withdrawal. He became evasive, deflecting questions, and his once temperate nature had given way to a cautious reticence. I found him texting a married female coworker habitually. When he snuck off to a beach to see her late one night, I was furious, and we argued. I was insecure; it was all in my head he said, as reality and fiction blurred and distorted. Words were weapons, slicing through what remained of my self-esteem with surgical precision. The sharp verbal blows left a million tiny cuts on my already fragile psyche. Fighting became more frequent, and I withdrew. Blocking the door, he backed me into corners – first, a push, then a shove. At first, I fought back. Lucas held me down on the bed by my hair, and I bit his chest before he released me. Shoving turned to hair pulling, slaps, and punches, lilac bruises blossoming beneath my skin, a sonnet of pain written in shades of purple and blue. Swollen lips were reminders of the battles lost, as I lay my armour down.

The nights were cold and dark, but everything looked far worse in the honesty of the morning light. He said sorry, his fragile words hanging heavy. He bought pink peonies, his eyes shimmering with regret. When I told him I was leaving, he begged me to stay. Small gestures, infused with sincerity, became the language of atonement, of contrition. I wanted to love him in a way that would heal us both.

For a fleeting season, the cold disappeared, the warmth returning. When his sun shone on me, it was glorious, and I felt it radiate on my skin. But the frost returned before the peonies wilted, and the last petals had fallen.

One night, he lashed out, and I fled to a local petrol station. A service attendant found me sobbing and led me out back. With an emerging black eye, a split lip, and my finger bent, bleeding, and swollen from bite marks, I was a broken mess.

Police arrived unexpectedly, their expressions concerned. Like a static rabbit caught in headlights on a dark road, I sat in shock on a milk crate in a storage room. The female officer soothed me, asking simple questions. Her partner, a tall and solid dark-haired man, hung back, studiously taking notes on a pocket-sized black notepad. When she had finished, he told me they would be applying for a domestic violence protection order on my behalf. His deep voice was firm but gentle as he told me it would help keep me safe. I bucked at the proposal, protesting, scared I would get Lucas in trouble.

The officer murmured with frustration.

'Sorry love. This is for your own good. You're not applying for it, we are.'

The officers drove me home in their patrol car and Lucas spent the night in the station lockup. As the hours tiptoed slowly toward the light, grief, a heavy metal, and anger, a fierce flame converged, volatile elements in alchemy, intricately intertwining. The sum of what we were changed that day. Barely sleeping, I couldn't look at him when he finally returned home.

A domestic violence order was granted – a piece of paper that asked nothing more of him than to be of "good behaviour," as though violence could be undone by a phrase. In the courtroom, I stood with my head down, ashamed. He didn't show up. Again, he said he was sorry, and he knew he needed help. His touch was tender and his steel-blue eyes full of pain and tears, swearing it would never happen again.

We saw a couples' therapist and began attending church. Starting afresh among those seeking atonement and the devoutly religious, I attempted to reinvent myself as unhindered by my grief. There was an intermission, a brief prelude in the conflict, but the following year, the battles continued. Any remaining tenacity had buckled. I'd been whittled away, peeled back to my molten core, my white flag waving.

The police returned, but each time I refused to press charges, throwing him a lifeline while I cast myself adrift. Those days were about survival in stormy seas, and I held on for dear life, ascribing nobility in my struggle. I let my body plunge down into dark, murky water while he swam through me, past me, beyond me. Drowning.

When survival becomes a delicate waltz of repetition, time moves slowly. Its movement is sluggish, like an abandoned shack in gradual decay. All around are unknown dangers, potholes, and pitfalls as it's slowly returned to nature. It becomes hard to see beyond there, what it once was and what it will be. You don't know the vulnerabilities, the topography — where to step to avoid perilous ground. I missed the warning signs, was careless. Then, one day, I stepped on a submerged landmine.

It started with a missed period when I was nineteen. Frozen by disbelief, I stood before the bathroom mirror, staring at the reflection of a woman whose life was spinning out of control. I was on contraceptives and yet... I prayed the double lines on my pregnancy test were an illusion of my imagination. The room echoed my sobs, and I reeled in shock. I cried into my work polo, staining the green cotton with black mascara.

Amid chaos, I faced a choice. A choice less like freedom and more a prison sentence. To keep the baby and bring it into my life, fragile as a house of cards, or to terminate the pregnancy, and carry the weight of guilt and regret for the rest of my life. For me, choosing whether to terminate this pregnancy was deciding between two awful choices.

At nineteen, I had little family support, no money, and an unstable relationship. I kept it secret at first, carrying the weight like a stone lodged in my chest. But secrets have a way of clawing their way to the surface, of demanding to be acknowledged. After a late-night call to a crisis pregnancy service, I hoped someone would throw me the lifeline, an answer that would make the decision process easier, lifting the shame and anxiety searing every part of me.

Growing up surrounded by religion and conservative values, my beliefs about sex, bodies, abortion, relationships, and gender roles were shaped long before I fully understood them. These ideas, deeply ingrained in me, felt like a fog that enveloped my instincts and gut feelings, becoming part of me on a cellular level.

When I was a little girl, my mother gave me the book The Atonement Child by Francine Rivers, a religious story of a young girl who is violently raped, becomes pregnant and decides to keep her baby and is blessed by God. It was a black-and-white absolute, there were no supplemental factors. Shame had been drilled into my bones since I was small, and I struggled to rid my body of that timeworn deadly and caustic marrow. This framework set the guilt, the self-condemnation and the shame that would blanket me years later.

However, it was reading that gave me flickers of opposing thought. On the contrary, I'd read many raw and emotional personal stories of women to understand the difficult nuances of such a decision; it was a gruelling choice and a decision that was rarely black and white. I held no antipathy to those making the decision to terminate, however, being pro-choice did not absolve me from the guilt that weighed so heavily on my conscience. I held no judgement of others, but that same compassion and mercy I could not yet extend to myself.

Lucas did not want the baby. I could see him in my mind, walking away and leaving me to raise her or him alone. We weighed the options, navigating the minefield of societal expectations, personal beliefs, and practical considerations. The decision before me was of two equally awful options, neither without long-lasting consequences.

Lucas drowned his anxiety in a bottle of scotch, declaring in a drunken mishmash of words he would not be a father again. There was no reaching him, no comfort, and no room for compromise. The terms of engagement were set.

The day I dreaded dawned, grey and heavy, the sky a mirror of the tumult raging within. We drove in screaming silence, the air thick with unspoken words and unshed tears. The health clinic loomed ahead, a blinding beacon of finality. Left at an old stone building, my mind raced, terrified it may be surrounded by protesters, like I'd seen on television, holding placards and shouting at me the condemnation I already felt for myself. Thankfully, it was eerily still except for the passing cars and wind, blowing autumn leaves across the footpath outside as I entered the lobby alone.

The waiting room was silent amidst the chaos of emotions

swamping me. Fluorescent lights hummed overhead, casting sterile brightness over the beige walls furnished with landscape paintings and brochures. I felt frightened. I wanted to be bundled up, taken home, and cared for, to be told everything would be okay. Yet here I was, grappling with the weight of choice, the heaviness of consequence.

As I waited in the reception area, I wailed silent heartfelt apologies to my belly and my hips. I admonished myself for being so goddamn weak. Pacing the boundaries of logic, I knew this was the only choice there was and that the life I lived was no place for a child.

I was called to see a counsellor. On the walls were diagrams of the female reproductive system, and posters of women smiling. She pulled out a notepad, made small talk and gave me a reassuring smile, noticing my discomfort and bloodshot eyes. We exchanged polite but hollow words. She asked deeper questions and I told her what she needed to hear. She then asked me why I wanted to have an abortion. Breathing deeply to control the tears suspended on the edge, I muttered something about being unable to look after a child and explained my relationship with Lucas. She then asked if he wanted a termination too. I nodded. She nodded and signed a form, tucking it into a folder.

She instructed me to again wait in the hallway. As I started to pick up a tatty magazine to distract myself, I heard my name called again. Entering a second office, a nurse put a band around my wrist and took my blood pressure, before tearing the cuff off and taking notes on a clipboard. She directed me to lie down where she performed an ultrasound: a tiny speck glowed on a black-and-white screen. Tearing off a small monochrome photo, she handed it to me. I froze, pulled under a riptide of anxiety, unable to breathe, overcome by anxiety and distress.

As if reading my thoughts, the nurse reassured me it's not a baby, it's a cluster of cells. Her words were supposed to turn something deeply emotional into simple science, existence into tissue and matter. She was so matter of fact about it, that I was carried along by her confidence. The journey to justify this act was a complicated one, a biology lesson where even science could not provide a black-and-white answer.

Taken to a changing booth, I pulled on a paper gown. I texted Lucas behind the curtain, desperately begging him to save me, to come and take me home. He offered vague encouragement and confirmation this was what we needed to do. We. As if he carried the weight of this grief too. He'd got off easy. This was my burden to bear.

I resented him for letting me face this alone. Conversations about the termination had been transitory and flimsy, brief interactions without substance, casual and curt, as though we were talking about the weather. I was a controlled burn, and he was a lone firefighter, keeping any hazard contained as it threatened to erupt and burn down a township.

I lay on the theatre table, staff in blue gowns, the sterile scent of antiseptic mingling with the tang of fear coating my tongue. A lamp overhead shone down like a harsh artificial sun. I sobbed as they inserted a cannular into my veins. The doctor warned me if I continued to cry, they would have to halt the procedure. I asked her if everyone felt this way. She answered bluntly, 'No'.

The memory reel cut out into the blackness. I couldn't assemble a scene from this amnesia. I drifted off into a fever dream and woke to a new world. When they wheeled me to recovery, I felt uneasy and dizzy, like I might pass out. In the bed next to me, there was a girl sobbing. They put her in a room and closed the door, but I could still hear her. The cramping was not too bad. They told me I should expect to bleed for at least a few days.

It's hard to put my finger on quite what I felt. Waves of emotional pain followed by another of respite so profound it left me breathless. I felt a need to cleanse myself, so as to wash away something invisible. A heaviness. Keeping up the rituals of normality was my best defence against grief. We got out of bed and ate breakfast at the kitchen table, going through the motions of the day as if it were any other. We don't speak its name, simply passing side by side without connecting, imagining it never happened. With grief, denial has its purpose. We stay hidden there, until we are ready to feel the pain. We can slip away, retreat and hibernate, put up a buffer to shield us from pain, but ultimately, there is no way but through it.

There was no space for hibernation of grief to lick my wounds, which felt like an indulgence. There was no room for the visceral reality of my loss. I began crying spontaneously when I was alone – little micro-cries that came up out of nowhere. Sometimes they subsided quickly. Sometimes I collapsed on the floor sobbing after getting home from work. I stopped eating properly. In the months following, I sought counselling for the loss. I kept the creased ultrasound in the pages of my diary for years after, unable to throw it out. In the lonely hours of the nights, shame, with its steady swing, oscillated through my body. I moved like a fatally wounded animal, crawling as far away from the pack as possible.

Something had slipped through my fingers. There was no catching it. I was so tired, but I couldn't sleep. Tossing and turning, I waited for the sun to rise. I wondered what, or who, those cells might have become – a he or she – should the pregnancy have transpired in another space or time.

I saw babies everywhere. I heard their cries in shopping centres and at the supermarket. Pregnant women with their swollen bellies and Huggies commercials delighting in the joy of being a mother. It was like they were taunting me, taking aim at my weakness, and striking me where it hurt. The grief was significant, a loss I chose but could not immediately recover from.

This period was low, melancholic. In grief, time ran slowly, like a trickling stream in a time of drought. It was geologic, moving so gradually, change was imperceptible. The days went on, feeling all the same. I rose for work, and the hours passing were a weary grind, and those I interacted with were a blur of indifference and triviality. Routine was noise, a willing distraction from a hopeless reality as guilt clawed at my beleaguered heart.

A year passed and there was little notable or admirable about this period. Repetition, it runs in a loop, circling and crossing over onto itself. He cast me out and wound me in, put me back together before throwing me against the wall. A willing hostage to an invisible string, my heart felt full of love when it wasn't suffocating.

A year later, I stood at a familiar ledge, peering over with fear.

My body knew something had changed before I did. Tender breasts and a heightened sense of smell, fatigue set in, and food tasted like ash on my tongue. I made an appointment at the clinic, but as the date approached, I couldn't bring myself to go through with another termination. Doing nothing was a choice in itself. Despite the daunting challenges ahead, I knew deep down that I couldn't bear to extinguish this tiny spark of existence.

Lucas lashed out, angry I decided to keep the baby, as though I had made the decision to spite him. I researched single parenting resources online, ready to take on parenting alone.

As I logged on, the search history revealed a dating site. Below this, there were three more. One brought up a profile. Country boy seeks girl to love.

I saw his profile picture; there was no mistake. I was red hot with fury; a lightning strike that could start forest fires. He followed me from room to room as I shut him out. Denials turned to explanations turned to justifications. When I told him I was done and gave nothing but silence, he threatened to punch me in the stomach and kill our baby. That was the tipping point.

Angry and numb, I screamed at him to get out. Soon, the house was silent.

He arrived at my workplace the next day with a smug look, informing me he had taken everything. When I returned from work, the house had been emptied of almost all our possessions. Sitting on the floor of the empty house, I sobbed. Twenty, pregnant, and alone. It was time to forge a new beginning.

I called Holly, needing a friend. We sat in my empty living room, and she helped me box up the little he left behind.

'What are you going to do, Mel?' she asked.

'I'm going to get up and survive. I'm going to love this baby, and we will be okay.'

Two days later, I pulled the door behind me for the last time. I could not afford to live there on my own, and now it held memories I could not separate from its walls. I rented a room in a shared house, concealing my pregnancy. I was not ready to face the truth, or the questions. Feeling uncertain — any glimpse of the future felt dubious now —

I became a creature of solitude.

Life continued around me, as people went on with their routines, scrolling on phones, drinking coffee, and reading the newspaper. I occupied a separate space, disconnected from the steady pulse of ordinary existence.

One morning, unable to sleep, I set out on foot, the weight of the world heavy. I found myself pulled into the cathedral a few blocks away. If God was anywhere, I hoped he might show up there. He and I had a lot to talk about.

Its majestic hardwood doors were open, welcoming those seeking refuge and sanctuary in this place of holy quiet. Light shone through the glorious stained-glass window, its ruptures of radiant colour across the altar. A delicate embroidered tapestry and prominent brass candlesticks towered above. Dark-stained pews smelled of wood and leather, and lavender filled the air.

Shame permeated every part of me, and I wondered if the guilt and sin I carried might set this sacred place alight. I sat on a pew, pulling my knees close to my chest. Fixated on the flickering candles over the altar, I fell into an almost hypnotic state.

Pain washed over like waves, pulling me to and fro. Hot tears spilt onto my cheeks, and I surrendered to the grief. I heard wailing like a wild animal, then recognised the inhumane wail as my own.

God help me.

Steadying my breathing as light filtered in, someone somewhere silently recited prayers that reached me, like little birds flying in through the dilapidated windows of my despair to perch in the archways of the filtered light, watching over me. I felt peace, an inner stillness, and a voice within whispering, 'Everything will be okay.'

I stepped out into the street, into the sunlight, with hope. For weeks, little miracles came, sometimes in disguise. I found an apartment. It was dark and ordinary, but it was mine.

My belly swelled, my nesting instinct overrode pregnancy

fatigue, and I cleaned and made the little apartment a home. I planted carnations and chrysanthemums in the little courtyard. After days of work, it was bright and clean.

I moved in with next to nothing. I didn't own a bed or television but slowly collected items for the baby with the little money I had. The kindness of others saved me, throwing me a lifeline that decades later I still think of with gratitude. Those little miracles landed on my shoulders like exquisite butterflies. Unbeknownst to me, a lady I had met at a young mum's pregnancy support group put out a call for assistance. Other women answered the call, bringing bags of baby clothes, furniture, and home-cooked meals. They offered words of encouragement and immense kindness to a stranger. They brought more than material things; they gave me hope.

By the time my baby was due to be born, the tired flat no one else wanted had become our home. I sat on the nursery floor, looking up at the white walls, patting my vast bump, surrounded by delicate blankets, pastel-coloured animals, and a tiny lamp casting soft shadows across the room. Little jumpsuits and tiny socks filled the dresser drawers. It was beautiful, and I felt overwhelming pride. I was strong, and I could do this. I was ready to be a mum. Another mother brought her newborn son around, and we sat talking for hours.

I looked forward to meeting my baby. After hearing my baby was a girl, I searched for a name and found one I loved. When I told a few people close to me, I was given a bright yellow cup with rainbow lettering: Lily. We had a name.

4

When Lily was born, her tiny frame nestling in my arms filled me with a love I never knew was possible. Her needs occupied my days and nights; there was more to life than myself. My daughter was everything, and I saw the future through a different lens.

As she grew, I grew as a person. Looking down into her pretty face and blue eyes overwhelmed me with a fervent desire to protect my child and give her the best life possible.

In the latter part of the pregnancy, Lucas returned full of remorse and promises. I was angry but did not want to keep my daughter from her father. Despite my hostility and distrust, he persisted, adamant he was a changed man and wanted to make amends, to be a father to our child. He would prove it; he would make it up to both of us, he promised, even if it took years.

I worked part-time, leaving us time together to explore and play. Lily was a curious child, fearless and intelligent. Those early days were magical with her little hand in mine.

Lucas would visit and bring toys. Things could have been better, but I could see he was trying. The aggression had gone and becoming a father again had changed him for the better.

Lily was eighteen months old when we moved in together as a family. Our new home was close to parks, bike paths, and lakes, and a perfect place for new beginnings.

Before long, the conflict began again, creeping up slowly, the nuances subtle and obvious to everyone but me. My friends knew I was in deep water despite my attempts to manage the optics. I didn't talk to them about what was happening behind closed doors because I didn't want to be rescued. I wanted to be a family. I was a willing prisoner. He was human cocaine, and I was an addict awaiting my next hit. I knew he was wrong but didn't know what was right.

Finally, I engaged with a counsellor for answers on fixing us, and fixing him, my nerves shattered, and my hands folded on my lap. Her office had folders stacked neatly on shelving, family photographs, and a miniature succulent garden next to lines of psychology textbooks. The walls held white framed degrees and inspiring quotes. She sat on an ochre sofa opposite me in a pressed pantsuit and sensible heels.

I confessed everything, spilling out like a storm drain after days of torrential rain. With our rental lease almost up, I had a choice about whether to renew and stay or pack our bags and go. Deeply unhappy, I pursued a quest for change. I wondered if the solution to this problem was in the rows of important-looking books. I was there for any answer except the one she gave.

'He can't change, and he won't change. The only one who can change your life is you.'

I faced an unexpected hurdle before I could make a choice.

'Congratulations, you're pregnant,' the nurse at my local doctor's office announced chirpily, her eyes bright with delight. When my eyes welled with tears, her expression was apologetic. I burned with sadness and fear. I'd hoped for another child one day, but not like this. The nurse held me soothingly as I cried, as I spilled my dilemma to a perfect stranger. She offered comfort and the telephone number of support services.

Leaving her office, I walked to a nearby park. With only the sound of birds and trees rustling in the breeze, I switched off my phone, rested on a swing, and stayed there for hours until the sun went down, afraid to go home.

When I did, Lucas refused to look me in the eye. He paced the room.

'Take care of this. I'm not paying for this kid.'

I met his eye, replying in a tone so still and measured, he looked on in disbelief.

'I don't need your help. I'm not asking for it. I've heard what you've said. You played a part in this, too. Again, it's up to me to deal with the consequences, but I will. I'm keeping this baby. If you don't want to be involved in its life, that's your choice. I will do this on my own.'

I sat on the front step of our house, taking some time and space to breathe. He retreated to the garage to tinker, smoke cigarettes, and cool off. There were no further arguments, no discussion, just stone-cold silence – space between two people.

I imagined a future alone with a young child and a baby on the way and asked myself why I had not learned the first time. Stupid girl, I chastised myself.

Days later, Lucas sat beside me on the front steps. The sunset blazed like gasoline. Red and orange. It was clear he had something on his mind. He rested a whisky glass on the concrete and lit a cigarette, the spiral of smoke curling as it caught the light.

I braced myself for an angry outburst or a guilt trip. What he said next caught me by surprise.

'I think we should move to the Gold Coast together as a family.

We can start a business, make some good money, and work on making things right. If you want us to keep the baby, that's okay. I love you, Mel, and I want us to be a family. I don't want to lose you.'

I couldn't look at him. My heart was sad, though this revelation glimmered of hope. I considered my choices over the coming days, struggling to decide. Afraid to go; yet scared to be alone. Being a single mum to two was an isolating thought. This could be the break we needed.

I found him in the kitchen. 'Okay, let's do it.'

It was a gamble; one I hoped would pay off. Our town felt like it was closing in.

Every place had history, porous and soaked in memory. The Gold Coast promised a clean slate. I could be a new human, untarnished by the past. This is the conundrum of those with stories too arduous to tell. Sometimes it is easier to let our old selves burn, and to reinvent ourselves unhindered. We packed our lives into a rented truck and began again.

At five o'clock in the middle of winter, I hugged the porcelain toilet bowl, trembling from the cold. Delicate frost patterns were etched on the window glass, tiles underfoot cool to the touch. Morning sickness had arrived with a vengeance.

I found a new job, intensified by a lengthy commute for training, and balanced parenting, housework, and Lucas's business paperwork at home. I forged ahead on sheer determination, beating off exhaustion, desperate to make things work. I walked a fine wire; things were manageable daily, but the meaningful change I had hoped for in our relationship had yet to come.

I saw moments of tenderness between other couples, their

closeness and connection evident. I longed for that type of relationship. It felt elusive, something not meant for me, like a little red bikini or wanting a pony when I was a child. I kept moving forward, trying to stay afloat and putting any discomfort down to an adjustment period, hoping it was something we would get through.

The Gold Coast was intimidating; the glitz of the glamour strip outshone me. Rows of hipster cafés by the beach, women wearing activewear, make-up, lashes, and perfect tans, their bleached ponytails swishing as they moved in packs.

The men, with sculpted biceps, tribal-style inking, and surf wear, sat around bar tables on the avenue. At night, the strip became a hunting ground for beautiful people. It took time to see beyond that view. I longed for deep conversations with good people. But with this desire came risk. With secrets to protect, I held back from getting down to the nitty-gritty, the brutal, raw honesty from which true friendships are born. They say no man is an island, but my social isolation was self-inflicted.

As my pregnancy moved through the stages, I hoped my efforts would pay off. Supporting Lucas's happiness felt like running a marathon, the finish line continuously shifting. As a final checkpoint was reached, another was added. Intrinsically, his self-worth was linked to material things where the dream felt unattainable, a mirage in the desert, a hunger that could never be satisfied. It didn't stop me from trying.

At twenty weeks pregnant, we learned Lily's new sibling would be a little sister, and soon after we moved into a larger house to hold our growing family. The first time I stepped inside, I felt a fragile optimism stir — the hope that these walls might shelter us, that this place could be home. There were sycamore trees, their mottled, paint-by-number bark. The leaves rusting and crisping at the edges, and abundant wildlife. Cockatoos and king parrots perched on the fence lines around the large backyard. There was room for a trampoline and swing set for the children.

Heavily pregnant, I prepared our baby's room. Tired, with swollen ankles, I was ready for the pregnancy to be over. My water broke on Valentine's Day, and I gave birth a few hours later. Cradling our newborn baby, I was mesmerised by how beautiful she was. We named her Ava. With her little hand wrapped around my pinkie finger as she slept, her long eyelashes fluttered like the wings of a tiny bird.

Lucas sent a bouquet of roses to my bedside. Leaving hospital the following morning, we adjusted to life at home, balancing time, money, and sleep. Exhausted from sleepless nights, I fought to keep it together. Lucas grew resentful of the increasing responsibility. As the only regular income earner, I had no choice but to return to work five weeks after Ava was born before we went under. Despite working long hours, we were in financial quicksand, pulled under the more we struggled. Knowing something had to change, I began studying nursing plus a second job at a supermarket to keep us financially afloat.

I hoped when Lily started school the following year, I would have a job with better hours and money. After days in classes and at work, I put the kids to bed and spent the evenings stocking shelves at our local supermarket. Putting my headphones in, I stacked cans and packages, the motions mechanical yet oddly soothing, an unspoken rhythm beneath the hum of fluorescent lights. In my mind, I was an architect drafting blueprints for a better tomorrow, each imagined corner a lifeline thrown across the chasm. Those daydreams were something tangible – threads of hope woven into the fabric of exhaustion.

One night, a few days before final exams, I put the children to bed and sat in the study to review course notes. Lucas returned from a neighbour's house, where he had gone to drink and unwind after work. The screen door thudded as he returned, and I heard him walk through the kitchen, knowing instinctively he wasn't in a good mood. I kept my distance.

'What's for dinner?' he asked.

'It's in the frypan. It's still warm,' I responded.

The study door opened, and he leaned against its frame, his face thundering.

'What are you doing? You're on that stupid computer again?' His words seared like a branding iron.

'I'm studying. I have an exam next week.'

As my eyes returned to my notes, he smashed the laptop, shattering the screen and knocking it to the floor.

'You're always on that fucking thing!' he shouted, storming out, the screen door clapping behind him, as I knelt to pick up the pieces. An hour later, Lucas returned.

'I'm sorry, baby. I'll get you a new one,' he promised, picking up the laptop and removing it from sight.

He pulled me into him, whispering he was sorry before kissing me. I could smell the scent of cigarettes on his shirt and taste the bitterness of stale beer on his breath. My nose was blocked from crying. I recoiled, hiding my repulsion to avoid making him angry. Deeply hurt, I retreated again down a rabbit hole of resentment. I knew he could see the fusion of pain and anger in my eyes. Staying angry would mean I had to do something. I would have to leave. I wasn't ready.

A period of platitudes and romantic grand gestures followed.

This was entirely predictable. He sent flowers and text messages telling me he loved me, did the washing, and took me out for dinner. His touch was tender as he spent days doing fun things with the kids, like a real family. Attentive and gentle, he was present and available until the smashing sounds and fear were a memory he had wallpapered over. Things felt good again.

I'd grown accustomed to the cycle. I rode the highs and endured the lows for yet another taste of the highs. Sometimes, they took months to come full circle. The good times we were a family, in love together, were a drug. It was an exhausting, disheartening existence, yet, in a way, intoxicating as I yearned for the happy moments. I lived for those days.

I graduated and began a new job in a local hospital where the pay was better, and I had flexibility with parenting responsibilities. I felt proud I'd achieved something worthwhile and found newfound confidence and happiness. A sense of purpose and pride. Good things started happening for me.

I began writing again because I had something to say. I sat in front of a blank page, with words like apparitions appearing in all directions. I chose the ones that spoke the loudest through the noise, piecing them together to create meaning from all the chaos. When one of the pieces was selected for publication, I shared the news with Lucas.

I sensed him inwardly wince with irritation. Uncomfortable with something shifting, like what I was telling him was a challenge, a personal affront. So, I stopped sharing good news.

I made myself smaller, folding myself up like origami, trying to take up less space, to not occupy any part of his spotlight.

Ava was six months old, and Lily nearly five. There were still details to iron out, but my new job at the hospital would allow me to be there for Lily as she started school, the new year months away. The girls grew up quickly, becoming more curious as they explored the world. Being their mother was the best thing in my life.

Closing my car door, I took a moment to gain my composure. I studied the symmetric building, one of several in a line like dominos; the stark whiteness of the wrought-iron bars on the windows, and the hardwood door, which was no different from any other in the row. With no signage, there was nothing unique about it, except a tiny flower emblem etched into the door, an intercom, and a security camera pointed toward the entrance.

I pressed the bell.

'Hello?' a polite female voice enquired through the speakerphone.

'Hi. My name is Melissa. I have an appointment today with Hannah. The hospital referred me,' I replied cautiously, my face flushed with embarrassment, thankful nobody else was around to hear.

There was a pause. 'Of course, come in.' Her tone was welcoming.

The door clicked and opened inwards, and a young woman standing on the other side smiled at me, gesturing for me to enter. 'I'm Hannah. I'm so glad you came.'

Her bright eyes were warm. They were green like a forest lake, but their intensity felt steadfast like an anchor. Her calmness stopped me from floating away with the riptide.

Hannah's fingernails were short and painted daffodil yellow. They matched the stitching of the Doc Martin boots under her skirt.

'Coffee?' she asked. I nodded, grateful.

As she reached for a coffee cup above the sink, I could see her arms as the sleeves of her tunic fell. Tiny, faded tiger stripes covered with bold, symbolic tattoos. I knew this was a girl who had stories. Those arms were a roadmap of the places she'd been, the things she'd seen, and the battles fought and won – the demons she had defeated in another lifetime.

As she prepared the coffee, we made small talk, conversation dancing on the surface. It lightened the mood. The white walls displayed children's artwork, brochures, and posters. Hannah handed me the coffee, and we moved to an upstairs loft. She summoned me into a cozy sitting room with a red woollen rug and a comfortable settee.

The room smelled of rose oil. I studied her face as she took a moment to read the clipboard she held. She wore a knee-length floral skirt, which revealed her graceful, willowy legs. I guessed she was in her early thirties. She bit her lip; her face focused with concentration as she studied the page.

Finally, she met my eyes, her expression curious and open. 'We received your referral from the hospital. They reported seeing you just a few days after Christmas. They were concerned you're not safe at home. Your partner assaulted you, and you've got stitches. How is the wound healing?' she asked cautiously, testing the waters.

My fingertips traced my upper lip, hitting tiny loops of plastic threading, my skin still weeping beneath. 'I'm doing okay, thanks. They come out in a week,' I replied, showing little emotion though my hands trembled.

She looked at me knowingly. 'Can you tell me what happened?'

'He got angry. I went to leave and he took our baby so that I couldn't go. He put her down to take some clothes I had packed. When I picked her up to leave, he punched me. My teeth split through my face.'

Her expression was one of concern. 'How long has this all been happening?' she asked, her voice empathetic and her eyes compassionate.

'Since 2001. It's been eight years now.' The reality of the declaration hit me. Where had all that time gone?

'He can be a good man and father, but I don't know him when he does things like that. It's torn our family apart.' I hadn't dared share this much detail with anyone; secrets locked up like Pandora's box, the weight of the burden exhausting. I was unwilling to bear people's judgement, but this woman seemed to understand.

'Things have been worse for the last year. I thought he'd beaten his demons. Our youngest daughter, she's nearly a year old now. We are struggling financially, and we're both tired. It's taken a toll on our family. I worry about the children.'

Hannah's gaze was intense; her hands folded in her lap. 'How so?'

'Well, things keep happening. I saw that look just eleven days after my youngest was born. You know the one I mean. The anger was incandescent. I knew what was coming. Things escalated – we had to go.' The words came out like artillery fire, sharp and rhythmic.

'He came at me. I almost dropped the baby.' My words started to fumble as I struggled to regain composure, feeling a sense of self-awareness of the horror revealed by the words I was speaking. I took a sharp breath.

'We left, staying at a nearby holiday park. The woman at the reception desk looked at us curiously because we arrived late at night and the address on my driver's licence was ten minutes away. She was supposed to turn us away – company policy. But she was kind. She saw me cradling a newborn and upgraded our room. I know she knew.' I listened to the words escaping a battered woman's mouth – my mouth. They offered no catharsis, no freedom.

I tried to picture my daughters, and a faint flicker of Lily emerged, her mousey brown pigtails and sky-blue eyes, like her father's, but bewildered and scared. Ava, still a toddler, had become clingy. Will they remember this when they're older? God, I hoped not.

I picked at my nails and stared intensely at an empty patch of wall, hoping to contain the emotion lapping at my insides and threatening to overflow. 'I feel like a freak, humiliated. I'm a nurse, and my workmates saw me covered in blood; they know now. They looked at me with pity. It was hard to take. I care for battered women, and I should know better. I feel ashamed that I'm stuck in this mess.'

'You're not alone, you know. Abuse isn't limited to any one type of person. We see everything from professionals, stay-at-home mums, older women, younger women, and wealthy women. It doesn't discriminate. One in three women experience domestic violence at the hands of a partner.'

'I get so caught up in trying to fix this… fix him.' I paused, my eyes focused on the seams of the settee as I traced them back and forth with my fingernails.

'He's had a rough childhood and a difficult relationship with his parents, bullied through school…' I explained as if it all made sense. 'He's still a bit broken. I hoped having a family who loved him would be enough to heal and change him.'

Hannah nodded. 'I've never met a perpetrator who doesn't see themselves as a victim,' she said pointedly. 'He's not a child anymore. It's up to him to take responsibility for his behaviour.'

I could only nod, thoughtful.

'He's agreed to go to counselling and to do a men's anger management program. I don't know if it will make any difference.'

It wasn't a fix, not yet, but it was the first time he'd said yes to help without resistance. Maybe, just maybe, it was a crack in the wall he'd built around himself.

'It's a start,' she answered.

Somewhere inside, a warning light had flickered to life. A sense of recognition stirred.

I'd been longing to ask several questions and now seemed a good time.

'Can he change? Can things get better? Is there anything I can do to fix this? I'm sure it's happened before, right?' I pleaded, my voice desperate.

Her eyes met mine, serious. 'Unfortunately, it's unlikely. I've never seen an abusive man change, at least not in the long term.'

I didn't like how she painted our future in shades of darkness.

'Unlikely? But not impossible though?' I questioned.

She frowned, looking at her feet. She seemed deep in thought.

'It's not impossible, I suppose. If an abuser was committed to changing and continued to work at it every single day...' she trailed off. She pulled out diagrams explaining how the cycle of violence began and continued. I heard every word she had to say. I understood, in theory, the gravity of her words.

Everything she was describing, the cycles, the patterns – she was reciting the lyrics of my life, a song I knew by heart. Although I was still in denial that what she said was relevant, I grasped the hope I was the exception. It was an inconvenient truth. I had two daughters at home. What would they do without a father?

It's not impossible. Her words lingered, giving me hope.

This revelation was a tiny spark of light in a sky of darkness. I clung to it. I needed hope, things would somehow fall into place. I would wake up, and this would all have been a bad dream. It would take some time.

Squalls of an early morning thunderstorm fell, and the rain drummed rhythmically on the rooftop. The wind sounded like crying animals and made the shutters vibrate, the water curling sideways across the panes. We lay under the covers in the warmth for hours, listening to the wind howl and whistle through the branches of the teak tree outside. Lily and Ava had woken us, startled by the weather, and we brought them under the covers between us, the four of us together in a king-size bed. Sheltered and secure, our pillows and blankets curved around us in a makeshift blanket and pillow fort.

The wind eased, and the rain slowed. Blue sky emerged slowly.

We decided to walk on the beach and buy the girls ice cream before sunset. The tide had turned, the choppy wash breaking over the water's edge, thrashing the rocks and sucking back in again, the ocean breathing deeply. The breeze carried the sea spray, which collected on my cheek, and sand grazed my ankles. It collected my hair, made it flow wildly, and made Lily's dress dance in the breeze.

The coolness of the afternoon air breathed new life into me. Lily held her arms out, her little hands curled around mine, and we leaned back into the earth and exhaled, our garments billowing like a ship's sail. The wind picked up and carried our laughter away. Because of the stormy weather, the sea churned, bringing driftwood, coral, and other treasures to shore.

Lily collected them in an orange bucket. She picked up sapphire and emerald-coloured pieces of glass smoothed by the ocean, spongey coral, shark eggshells, mother-of-pearl shell pieces, cuttings of nylon rope, and flat, curved stones. She beamed as she held her finds.

Lucas crouched on the damp sand, Ava stood before him digging her toes in, spellbound by the sensation. I watched his face, his tanned skin and stubble. He was barefoot, his eyes closed, and his face turned towards the sunshine. Ava smiled a toothy grin and reached to pat his cheeks. He laughed, opened his eyes, and scooped her up, lifting her over his head. He could be so effervescent when he wanted to be, when all was quiet and it's just us. I joined him and sat on the sand. Ava wobbled her little legs between my knees, holding on to get her balance, her eyes alight and smile wide. Lily tipped the contents of her bucket on the sand.

The girls chatted playfully to each other. Lucas sat behind me and pulled me in, my back to his chest, my head on his shoulder. I could feel his warmth, his breath, and his heartbeat over the roar of the surf. Squeezing my hand, he didn't have to say a word. This was a language I knew.

We gazed at the sky. Its pink, amber, and gold mottle settled on the horizon as the sky faded to a powder blue. Cloud lay low, and the sun's golden disc slipped down into the sea.

5

Holly leaned against the back of the old Ute, the cold metal against the skin of her shoulders making her flinch, giggle, and gasp, sliding forward on the tray and adjusting the cotton blanket draped over her slender legs. She had named her car Clyde, her grandfather's middle name. He had given the car to her when his health deteriorated, and he could no longer drive.

He'd looked after it meticulously for decades, the timeworn leather seats still intact, the old-style gauges immaculate. On nights like this, I knew why she loved it so. Clyde had character. We set out, driving the ocean roads of the coast, making our way to a familiar place on a headland.

After navigating sandy tracks and scrubland, we arrived and set a campfire. Holly pulled off her boots, tossed them aside, undid her long hair from its bounds and let it fall down her back. We looked out, the land outstretched and bleeding into the sky like watercolour.

I could feel the hint of salt on my lips, the crash of the surf roaring below, the expanse of the nightscape concaving around us from the back of Clyde's open tray, and tiny fires burning brightly in the sky above us. The air was fresh; the cool breeze blew wisps of hair across our cheekbones. We watched the deep, dark blue sea below, reflecting the milky spray of stars above.

Pulling out a worn yoga mat, we made ourselves comfortable. The earth before us crackled a roaring fire built from fallen branches, its heat radiant. Its blue and orange flames danced together like the energy of two lovers colliding. The charcoal embers fluttered to the ivory sand below. Burnt eucalyptus leaves scented the air. I gazed at the lights of the houses lining the coast below, flicking on, mimicking the stars in the sky but constellations of human desolation. My eyes followed the lines forming streets, the grids speckled with yellow lights holding homes filled with people I'd never met.

As Hannah's words lingered, I wondered which were statistically unlucky, which houses were tainted with the same angst and sorrow, and the same confusion I felt. Staying with my parents, I had found myself on their doorstep shortly before midnight, the girls in the back seat with their clothes, blankets, and pillows. My eye was swollen, the skin an ugly shade of plum. My parents dared not ask questions.

Perhaps sensing my need for distraction, Holly switched on the radio with a cheeky smile, singing along to a Beyoncé track. She threw aside a blanket and dangled her legs over the tray's edge, the fire's glow reflecting on her tanned skin.

'Look at those stars, they're beautiful,' I said whimsically, filled with a sense of awe. A breeze brought goosebumps to my skin, and I shivered slightly. The night was glorious.

'I've been thinking.'

'Oh?' Holly asked with curiosity.

'Everything that's happened at home lately has turned me upside down. There was a woman I cared for at work last week. She was twenty-nine. She was a mother; she had a little boy. Her mother had taped pictures of her with her family and friends on the wall. They were photos of her at Christmas, travelling to incredible places, just living her life to the fullest. I looked at the snapshots. She was beautiful. The light in her eyes had gone out, her stare now vacant. When she went for surgery to reduce the swelling in her skull, they had shaved her beautiful blonde locks. I almost didn't recognise her. Gaunt and pale, with dark circles under her eyes, a shell of who she was, her speech was slurred and slow. Her son sat on her bed gazing at her, confused, like he didn't recognise her. He was looking for his mother, but she had gone away. It broke my heart. I read her case notes. Her boyfriend beat her, and she had a brain bleed. She can't walk or shower herself. We feed her with a spoon. Such a beautiful girl, what a fucking waste.'

I felt a pang, a recognition I didn't want. Was that the shadow of myself I recognised in her suffering? A voice in the back of my mind whispered doubt, fear, the old chains tugging at me. Could I end up like her? Or worse, cling to the life I hated because leaving felt impossible? My nervous system was in tatters.

Holly nodded, laying her chin on her folded arms as she listened.

'I thought about it, and something hit home. Is that me? Could that be me? I used to be strong and determined. I wanted my daughters to look up to me and I wanted to show them how to live happy lives. I was going to do something meaningful with it. Now I'm lost. I don't even know what's true anymore.'

Holly adjusted her skirt and brushed her hair from her face. She nodded, waiting for me to finish. Her brow creased as she considered her answer. 'The truth is what you save from the fire, Mel. What you fight for, even when it's really fucking hard. Find out what you're worth, then hold it tight and let the rest burn. You'll teach those girls to know that no one's perfect. I learned that it's okay to make mistakes and fall sometimes. Then you stand back up and keep trying. He's made you feel guilty because you feel sorry for him. You deserve better, and you will come out of this with so much power and strength that you won't even know yourself.'

She met my eyes.

We stared at each other, a quiet knowing.

'You are strong. You're still learning your worth. One day, this will be all behind you. I know there's so much out there for you. You just must look after yourself and the girls first. Have faith. Tomorrow knows what tomorrow knows.'

Her words sat between us, glowing like the fire, both comfort and challenge. I wanted to believe them, wanted to see myself in the strength she described, but the pull of doubt was still strong, tugging at me like an undertow. Part of me clung to the hope she offered, fragile as smoke, while another part fought against the fear of what it would mean to finally let go.

I slowly let out the breath I had been holding.

'God, I hope so.'

It was a rainy, cold, and overcast Tuesday afternoon, and our local theme park, usually swarming with tourists, was deserted. The rollercoasters' mechanical clacking and the screams of riders could be heard over the rain. The weather was perfect for us. It meant no lines.

Our wet weather ponchos flapping in the breeze, we ran towards the carousel. Its vibrant lights flickered against the dusky sky, casting a kaleidoscope of colour across the park. The hypnotic melody, a whimsical tune, carried on the breeze as the skies gave way yet again, dull thunder echoing in the distance.

The girls climbed onto a majestic horse, painted in hues of crimson, gold, and royal blue. Bejewelled with ornate details, their manes frozen mid-gallop, the carousel whirled to life, into a realm where time stood still.

Their laughter was like a cascade of tiny bells, each peal brighter than the last, ringing out in pure, unrestrained joy. It bubbled up from their chests, a sound so light and airy that it seemed to dance on the wind. The giggles came in waves, sometimes breathless, sometimes bursting with energy, filling the air with a warmth that was almost tangible. The sound was as infectious as it was innocent, the kind of laughter that made the world seem brighter, as if the very sound of their happiness could chase away any shadow.

The rain fell heavily around us as the merry-go-round turned; we were lost in colours, lights, a melodic ballad playing. I took in the moment. Every detail was perfect.

The humidity from the ponchos, the tiny droplets of rain running down my daughters' hair, how they glowed. The delight on their faces filled me with joy.

In days past, I may not have noticed these details with such clarity. In the quiet depths of introspection, I found myself grappling with what truly mattered. Something had shifted, leading me to reassess things I'd taken for granted.

A few weeks before, while working at a small hospital, I came across a young colleague in tears. She hid away in a disused bathroom, but I heard her sobs. As I found her, I saw her eyes, swollen and teary. Her wet brown locks clung to her face. She caught my eye, startled, fighting to pull herself together. I stood alongside her, reaching out my hand.

When she spoke, she said something that entirely unzipped me, piercing me right to my core.

'I've been trying to have a baby. I just got a call from our fertility nurse. It failed again.'

I listened quietly, unsure of how to answer. Her lip quivered; her sadness was emphasised in every word.

'This was our seventh try. I can't understand why it's not working. I'm so tired. I don't know how to tell my husband.' She blinked back tears. Her shoulders heaved as she sobbed. I had no comforting words to ease her pain. We moved to a courtyard wooden bench surrounded by amaryllis flowers.

'I don't feel like a real woman. He should leave and find someone who can give him a child. He'd make such a good dad.'

She leaned forward to rest her head in her hands and I let her cry. Every part of me ached with compassion for her pain. I wished I could make it go away. But compassion is not about having answers, instead, about giving all the love you've got. I wished I could offer the baby she desperately wanted, but this was bigger than me.

Her sadness followed me like a dark shadow over the coming days. I noticed her go about her work as she cared for others, keeping distracted enough to get through the day. The energetic woman we knew had gone to ground, and in her place a woman lost in grief, longing for a child she wasn't sure would come into her life.

I watched on as she tended an elderly patient. Straightening his collar, combing his thin, greying hair, talking to him softly about the photo of the little Yorkshire terrier on his dresser. I saw her capacity to love, and it felt cruelly unfair.

My children came easily; this realisation came with guilt.

Watching her pain, stirred something profound inside me, and a seed was sown. Soon after, she unexpectedly relocated to a city hospital when her husband accepted a job promotion. We didn't stay in touch, but her courage to share her vulnerability moved me to action.

In the staffroom days later, holding a cup of instant coffee, I sat, lost amongst the chatter of television infomercials, making the most of the time I had before I was due back on the ward. I flipped through the pages of a discarded newspaper. There, a small picture of a stork and baby caught my attention. Mistaking it for a birth announcement, I read the words printed in an elegant italic font:

Egg Donor Wanted: We are a loving couple looking for a kind and compassionate young woman to help us to have a family. After many attempts of IVF without success, our fertility specialist has advised us to look for an egg donor in hopes we might experience parenthood together. If you are between 18 and 38, healthy, and would consider helping us, we would like to hear from you.

How unusual. I'd never heard of egg donation. My break ended and I rose to leave, tearing the advertisement from the newspaper and tucking it into my pocket. Later, I retrieved it, smoothing the ragged edges, showing it to a fellow nurse.

'How many people do you think would respond to an ad like this?'

She leaned over, reading carefully, biting her lip. 'Oh… I'd say maybe a few,' she said thoughtfully.

I shrugged, a hesitant smile brushing my lips. 'Well, I guess they won't want my eggs then.'

There would be girls younger, prettier, smarter than me. Women willing to give. I tucked the thought away.

But curiosity flickered. That night, in the dark silence of the house, I typed 'egg donor Gold Coast'. A stream of results spilled across the screen: pleas for help, for generosity, for hope. In Australia, donation was altruistic, unpaid. Few offered, many waited. Years could pass before a match.

The first ad was from a couple named Charlotte and Andy: "*After a decade of trying everything to conceive, our only chance is through egg donation. We seek a generous, empathetic woman in Southeast Queensland, or elsewhere, to help us.*"

Their words painted ordinary magic: a collie in the chewing phase, a house by the sea, shared joys, small routines. I read dozens of ads, my chest tight with quiet longing. The "hundreds of women" I once imagined didn't exist. Some waited years for a single reply. At twenty-seven, healthy, my age a rare commodity, I could help.

I returned to Charlotte's ad again and again, drawn to the life behind her words. I wrote:

"Dear Charlotte, it was lovely to read your ad. I'm twenty-seven, a nurse from the Gold Coast. I have a partner and two daughters, aged five and one. I love being a mum and would love to help someone else experience this. You seem like lovely people who would make great parents. I would love to talk about the possibility of becoming your donor."

Soon, a reply:

"Mel, thanks for your message. It's lovely to meet you. We would love to chat and get to know each other better."

Over days, our emails wove a tapestry of cautious hope. She sent a photograph, and I studied it, searching for the hidden story. Her forum diary, eighteen months long, chronicled setbacks, triumphs, two potential donors lost to circumstance – but through it all, her optimism never faltered.

"Can we meet for coffee? It would be nice to meet in person."

Two days later, I arrived at the café, a swirl of scent and chatter, people cradling cappuccinos, voices warm and low. I paused at the bathroom, checked my hair, whispered courage into my reflection. Doubts gnawed: Will they like me? Will they even want to make a baby with my eggs? What if they're expecting someone else?

I silenced the questions. I could step away. They could not.

Charlotte appeared first, sandy hair falling like sunlit waves over her shoulders. Her eyes met mine and held me there, crinkling gently at the corners when she smiled, alive with story – pain and joy stitched together, the depth of loss and the breadth of hope. In those eyes, I glimpsed a woman who had survived brutal blows yet still knew deep love and untamed hope. Andy followed, tall, open, warmth radiating from his easy smile.

'It's lovely to meet you finally,' she said, voice soft, eyes twinkling.

The nerves melted. Words flowed. Stories spilled across the table – doctors' bleak predictions, the long wait, heartbreak. We laughed about Rex, their mischievous collie, destroyed shoes, a ruined couch. Andy's eyes glimmered as he spoke of surfing and skating; Charlotte's words held steadiness, warmth, light.

They asked about me.

'What made you want to donate?' Andy's curiosity hung in the air.

I paused, considering.

'I have two great kids. Our family is complete. I'm twenty-seven and don't need my eggs anymore. I have something I don't need that could help someone else. Why not? When I saw your ad, I could tell this matters to you. I want to help.'

Charlotte's eyes filled, the quiet swell of emotion tender and raw. She was silent, and I felt the weight of everything she had endured, every hope and heartbreak woven into the glimmer of her gaze. I went home, mind spinning, touched by the generosity and courage I had seen. They were who I had hoped for.

That evening, I spoke to Lucas. He nodded, asking only what he needed to do: sign a form, tell the counsellor he was okay. Simplicity. While he understood, I sat back, reflecting on the quiet miracle of that meeting, the strange, luminous magic of offering something I did not need to someone who needed it more than anything.

Talking to my children was different. Ava was too young to understand, but Lily could grasp the idea if explained in simple terms. Our conversation began on that rainy afternoon at the amusement park. Relaxed in each other's company, I introduced the topic with Lily.

'Mum is lucky to have great kids I can do fun things with,' I started. 'Did you know not everyone can have kids?'

'Why not?' Lily asked, her expression curious.

'Well, some ladies don't have eggs to make babies, or their eggs don't work. They need someone else to give them some eggs so they can be mums and have kids.' I pointed to a garden bed of thousands of tiny, white stones. 'See those pebbles? That's how many eggs Mum has. I don't need my eggs anymore because I'm happy with having two beautiful girls. My friend Charlotte, she doesn't have any.'

Lily seemed to ponder the information for a moment before perking up.

'If you have lots of eggs, why don't you share some?'

'That would be a nice thing to do, wouldn't it?' I smiled. Later that day I phoned Charlotte and told her I would love to be their donor.

While it seemed like it was a simple decision to make, there was a lot of contemplating that occurred. There was the ethics of embryos – those that thrived, and those that could be discarded, little question marks, a tiny chance of unknown quantities, understanding things could fall together at the right time and a life could begin.

There was also the discussion, factored in by my religious upbringing, that questioned when life truly began. Was it with a fertilised embryo? An embryo that implanted into a uterine wall? At the presence of a heartbeat? At the stage of pregnancy viability? Birth? These were questions of science and ethics, and the answers were varied and subjective, in the same way the nurse at my termination had labelled my early pregnancy just a 'cluster of cells'. Science was a complex game and people often argued that just because we can, it doesn't mean we should. I understood this and took the time to explore what I believed and what was right. I still felt some regret from not proceeding with my first pregnancy and considered this could be atonement for it in some diminutive way. I believe you can be both pro-life and pro-choice simultaneously and this was one of the many things I had pondered during this period.

In December 2009, two months after I'd offered to donate, I sat with Charlotte and her husband in their doctor's office. The pastel walls held pinboards of cards, photographs of newborn babies and pregnant bellies, the collective outpouring of gratitude.

Our specialist was a brilliant, playful man who lightened the dense mood. We filled in paperwork, and I underwent an ultrasound. He produced forms for blood tests, checking for infectious diseases and genetic abnormalities. He informed us that if clear, we would be ready to start by the new year.

Our next appointment was a group session with a counsellor. She had green cat-like eyes and ash-grey hair. I guessed she was in her early sixties. She wore a brightly coloured floral dress with a unique necklace matching her bold eye shadow. I complimented her on it as we entered her office.

'Thank you, my granddaughter made it for my birthday. She's seven. A fashion designer in the making.' She winked as we sat on the sofas, ready to begin.

They wanted to know if I had thought through my decision. Would I wake up one day and have regrets? Did I know what I was doing? Over the next hour, we discussed topics like future contact and how to tell a child about their donor origins. We weighed up possible outcomes, how we might feel if things didn't go as we hoped. The donation did not promise a baby, but there was always hope. The relief on Charlotte's face as we left the clinic was evident. If everything came back normal, I could donate after Christmas. Weeks later, we got the approval that we were ready to go.

The new year arrived, and the process began. Daily injections would stimulate my ovaries to produce eggs within small follicles. The doctor would track the growth until they were large enough for the eggs to be collected. Pleased with what he saw during routine scans, the day to retrieve them was set.

I awoke early, having barely slept. The hopeful parents-to-be came early to drive me to the clinic. On arrival, we completed routine health checks, and an anaesthesiologist inserted a cannular in preparation for theatre. Charlotte's face registered fear, awe, and guilt all at once as she looked at me. A young nurse handed me a theatre gown and waited as I changed before directing me onto an awaiting bed and wheeling me to theatre across polished floors.

The room glowed clinical white and smelled of disinfectant. Gleaming stainless-steel surfaces created an aura of sterility. Nurses moved about with practiced precision, explaining the doctor would write the number of eggs collected on my hand for when I woke. A syringe of clear liquid was inserted into the cannular, crawling through my veins, and the world went dark.

I woke in the recovery ward, drowsy. As I came to, I remembered what the nurse told me about looking for a number. Lifting my heavy hand to my face, I concentrated, bringing focus to a still distorted world.

Twenty-two.

Resting in recovery under a warm blanket, I felt a sense of achievement. A nurse handed me my phone, and I sent a message to Charlotte. She was outside, awaiting news.

'I'm awake. We got 22 eggs!'

My phone vibrated with her reply.

'That's incredible! Hope you're feeling okay.'

My arms were heavy as the anaesthetic wore off, my abdomen tender and bruised, but otherwise, I felt good. Charlotte was let in to see me. She asked me how I was. There was a softness in her eyes. She thanked me over and over. I could see relief unspoken, but also another part of her – the part that was afraid and wasn't truly yet ready to exhale.

In March, she transferred two embryos.

Ten days later, she called as I drove my mother to the airport. 'It's positive, Mel! I'm pregnant! I can't believe it!'

My breath caught, bursts of glee tumbling from my soaring heart, spilling out in laughter and excited shrieks I could no longer contain. My mother, who could not hear the conversation, gave me a look that said I'd lost my mind, but I didn't care.

It wasn't just joy for them. It was the fragile, luminous hope I had carried and offered. I felt it rise in me, a quiet miracle, knowing I had helped create a chance at life, a dream fulfilled.

In their happiness, I glimpsed something deeper in myself – an understanding that giving hope could touch more than one life. It was a joy threaded with trust, courage, and the strange, searing satisfaction of being part of something larger than myself.

I realised the joy wasn't only for the outcome, it was for the act of giving, for the chance to offer life in a way I could never have imagined. For the first time, I understood that parenthood, in all its forms, isn't limited to my own children. That moment carried weight and wonder – that this small, miraculous joy belonged not just to them, but to me as well.

I had been invested in their success, bonded with her in ways for which I had no language, no vocabulary, no measure. I had walked with her in and out of light, carried hope alongside her. I blinked, and my eyes became a river breaking its banks. Here was the opening of a thousand unwritten days, the spark of everything that was yet to come.

This was a defining moment. The news vibrated between us with intensity; fragile, cautious, threaded with wonder. It wasn't just their happiness; it was the quiet miracle of giving hope, returned to me in waves of awe and gratitude.

At twenty weeks, they learned they were expecting a baby boy. Her belly swelled, and my chest fluttered with awe, with something I could hardly name.

This new life was theirs, yet I felt the weight of its unfolding. Would his arrival change the bond we'd begun to weave, or deepen it? In that anticipation, I felt the strange alchemy of giving and being changed at once, life unfolding through us all.

It was a question I had first encountered long before, while scrolling through forums late at night. I read stories of others desperate for an egg donor, and it became almost impossible to sit still, to do nothing. Each story carried weight, each desire was a life trembling on the edge of hope. Since a donation could create a connection for life, I felt the responsibility acutely – for myself, for my children, and for the child who might come from it.

Not all donations were smooth. Not every intended parent was like Charlotte. I had heard the tales of donors left hollowed, shattered after an ultimate act of generosity. One woman, after giving the most intimate part of herself, was ushered into a taxi and told she would never see or hear from the child or the parents again. Others disappeared, keeping the donation a secret from everyone, including the child.

Not every donor wanted contact, but every donor wanted honesty. And not every donor received that.

Humans and their emotions are rarely tidy, rarely kind.

I saw the red flags and wondered if I'd be so lucky next time.

And yet, I wanted to do it again. The experience had been one of hope – perhaps the first time I ever truly felt capable, truly good at something. It was easy, in a way that surprised me, almost involuntary, as if my body already knew what to do. And it mattered. It gave life meaning – not only to the women I helped, but to a part of myself I had long thought wasted.

It was light in the darkness. A rush of hope that hit like dopamine, a reminder that even in the most jagged corners of my life, I could create something beautiful. My body held opposites:

pain and invisibility, and yet the capacity to give, to create meaning, to birth a new life from the depths of my own ordinary existence. It was sharp and soft all at once, the kindness and empathy I could offer forming edges porous enough to let love through.

I sensed something miraculous, fragile yet immense, unfolding in the quiet. A new beginning, not just for the women I helped, but for me too. This experience was a kaleidoscope of contrasts – a river carving a path through rock, relentless and transformative, shaping something that would endure. And in that, I found a reason to do it again.

Human lives unfolded like a television series, and I watched, a voyeur of their triumphs and tribulations. Each story wove a tapestry that drew me closer, threads of joy and suffering entwining with my own pulse. Their victories lifted me; their pain sank into me. Vulnerability glimmered like light through glass, revealing the fragile threads of shared humanity and the quiet need for hope that binds us all. I became invested, carried along by their resilience, and the desire to help swelled within me, fierce and unshakable.

Lucas had been attending counselling sessions for a few months. He was calm, helping with the dishes, caring for the children, and sending loving text messages. We attended a few couples counselling sessions and were upfront about the abuse. Lucas shared his childhood traumas, letting himself be vulnerable. I had not seen this side of him in years. The counsellor advised he should work with Lucas independently. He enrolled into a group class for men. It seemed to make a difference.

Then, I felt a shift. He wore a black t-shirt with the slogan 'my anger management class pisses me off' to a counselling session. While cleaning the garage, I found a course worksheet with one question answered. It asked if hitting a woman was ever acceptable. In his handwriting on the top line, he had written: 'Only if the bitch deserved it.' When I found it, I was devastated. I confronted Lucas, and he laughed and told me it was a joke between the boys, and I needed to lighten up. The little voice whispering to me that something wasn't right soon began to scream constantly into a void.

I stood at the crossroads many times, crushed by indecision. His self-esteem was wounded, and I was worried a betrayal would destroy him, and he in turn would destroy me. I wasn't oblivious to who he was, he showed me every day. I convinced myself he loved me or at least had the capacity to love, and he one day would. He needed me.

I knew if our relationship was to work out, I'd have to adjust my expectations: to love and accept him for all his brokenness and make allowances. Look the other way. Get over it. Again, and again, and again.

In October 2010, spring reawakened flowers and trees and word was received that Charlotte and Andy's baby had arrived, making his entrance into the world ahead of schedule, but both he and Charlotte were flourishing. She invited me to come visit them at the hospital. My insides danced with nerves, a medley of butterflies scattering as I planned to meet their child, one who also shared half of my genetic makeup.

Entering the hospital, I was like an anxious teenager embarking on a first date, clutching flowers. As I neared the maternity wing, I felt a surge of apprehension. Finding their room, I took a moment to compose myself. Before I could utter a word, Charlotte's gaze met mine, a radiant smile gracing her lips as she rose to embrace me. 'Mel! How are you?' Her voice enveloped me in warmth, instantly easing my nerves.

'I'm great. More importantly, how are you?' I replied, searching her weary yet contented expression for clues.

She seemed tired but at peace. 'We are all doing wonderfully. Meet baby Will,' she said, nudging his crib towards me. Peering down at the tiny bundle before me, I marvelled at his perfection. Studying his delicate features, I sought something familiar, perhaps a resemblance to my own daughters. To my surprise, there were none.

Was Charlotte unsettled by my presence? I scrutinised her demeanour for any hint of discomfort, but aside from the weariness accompanying new mothers, there was nothing. If she harboured any unease, she concealed it well.

Turning my introspection inward, I probed for unexpected emotions. Was there a bond? No. Did I feel regret? None whatsoever. Akin to admiring a friend's child, I understood the genetic connection, but this child was not mine. I hadn't felt his kicks in my belly or heard his heartbeat.

Yet, I was overwhelmed by joy, contentment, and honour. Andy entered the room, greeting me with a hug. I observed their happiness as they beamed at their baby from the side of his cot. Leaving the hospital, pride washed over me. This day marked the beginning of their journey as a family; one I'd helped set into motion.

6

It was a hot afternoon in the bustling streets of Chiang Mai, in the hilly northern region of Thailand. We wandered the streets of the local night bazaar, the clattering of stalls echoing through the lanes as workers prepared for the tourists that would descend as the sun went down. As night fell, the markets illuminated with coloured neon lights, the exotic flavours of Thai cooking emanating from nearby restaurants, permeating the air as the quiet streets came alive.

The following morning, we hired a driver to take us to an elephant conservation park. Seeing the elephants was the girls' favourite thing to do and we went to admire the beautiful animals every time we returned to the city.

Under a hefty bamboo bridge, the elephant herd bathed in the river below. Their handlers scrubbed the elephants' muscular bodies with a stiff brush, their ears flapping with pleasure as they lazed in the rushing water. My daughters laughed excitedly as the elephants rose from the water, their trunks reaching to greedily snatch bundles of bananas and bamboo from our outstretched hands.

Young village women worked on the nearby riverbank, selling postcards and souvenirs while happily chatting to the children in broken English.

My parents had recently moved to Chiang Mai, initially for only a period to do volunteer work, but then fell in love with the country and its people. My mother taught at a school, and my father at a drug and alcohol rehabilitation facility. They had grown tired of the repetition of life in Australia, working hard but feeling like they were getting nowhere, and decided to move to Thailand.

At that time in my life, I could empathise. Routine was dulled by the weight of monotony, every task a chore, each day an endless repetition of the last. I felt blessed to have my children but often overwhelmed by the responsibility of being a parent, to be able to give them the time they deserved.

After we arrived, I struggled to be fully present, the weight of what I'd read pressing on my back. Fertility forums and donor groups had become a storm cloud that shadowed me, a tide of stories that rippled through my consciousness. Most were luminous with hope – glimpses of connection, flickers of gratitude, the quiet joy of giving life. Each story a fragile filament of gold, a reminder of why people gave: to offer light, to create meaning, to touch the deepest desire of another human soul.

But the world of donation was never simple, never purely light. Some recipients vanished the moment a pregnancy was confirmed, leaving donors suspended in hope that evaporated like mist. Others ghosted after the cycle, or reached out only in fragments, leaving donors to wonder if their gifts had ever mattered. One thread told of a recipient who kept a donor on Facebook but nothing more – a faint, trembling tether, while the child grew unseen and unshared. Another recounted a donor whose medication had been altered by the clinic after previous successes; a failed transfer was met with silence for a year, only for a cold message to arrive about a second frozen embryo. The uncertainty, the lack of communication, the quiet manipulations – it all lay bare and brittle as a winter tree stripped of its leaves.

Some stories struck sharper still, visceral in their cruelty. A donor abandoned hours after her collection because the recipient doubted her partner. Another recoiled in fear that a child might resemble the donor too closely, withdrawing entirely. In every post, I saw health risks ignored, costs unpaid, grief folded into invisibility. A slide of hand, a trick of light – hope seemed solid, and then it vanished. The pain for some donors felt like a soaring bird smashing into glass, sudden and shattering. The ambivalence of some intended parents, eyes fixed only on a prize, hit like a speeding train. Ghosted messages, broken promises, withheld contact – these threads ran like shadows through the golden tapestry of hope.

And yet, hope endured. For every thread of despair, there were glimpses of gratitude, of tangible connection, of lives forever changed. That fragile light pulled me forward, reminding me that giving – truly giving – could lift others, and lift me along with them. Even in a world jagged and unpredictable, even when the exceptions cut deep, the act of offering hope remained its own quiet miracle.

I read these accounts, absorbing joy and heartbreak alike, learning that hope was never guaranteed, but always worth the risk. And still, despite it all, I wanted to help. Because the possibility of light, of meaning, of witnessing life unfold – that was why I gave, and why I would give again.

It required a shift in perspective, a willingness to see the good, to view the bigger picture through a lens of hope. Yet, I also knew I needed distance.

Social media, the endless threads and interactions, had swallowed my attention, becoming an almost addictive pulse I couldn't escape. It was time to step back, to reclaim my priorities.

And so, I unplugged. I was a digital junkie in detox. My virtual skin itched. I jittered, wrestled with the fear of missing out, my chest hammering like a blacksmith at the forge, each beat urgent. Then, slowly, the weight lifted. The air cleared. I felt unburdened, clean.

Freed from the noise, peace returned in ways I hadn't felt in years. I spent my days wandering the streets of the northern city, letting the sunlight and sea breeze reset my mind, redefining who I was and what I stood for. And when my holiday ended, boarding the flight home felt less like a return and more like a quiet, necessary rebirth.

I'd been searching for my purpose, my place in the world. I spent countless hours untangling what I truly wanted, struggling to separate my identity from my passion for donation and my conviction that change was needed. I had waited, hoping someone else would take the lead, but slowly it became clear that if anything was to happen, it would have to be me.

At that time, I wasn't ready for the hard work I knew would be inevitable. I felt like an average person, nothing special, adrift, unfamiliar even to herself – damaged, uncertain of my own strength or resilience. I wanted to be liked; I craved validation, fully aware that taking action would invite criticism. Fear clung to me: fear of judgment, of ridicule, of failure. I didn't truly know myself. And yet, even as doubt fluttered through me, something that mattered to me began to pull me forward, gently lifting me from the shadows of my own fear.

Six months after disconnecting from social media, a gentle

prod emerged – small, insistent. I allowed myself to breathe, to think, to let the ideas grow. And as they grew, so did I. In the quiet, I began to recognise my own resilience, the strength that had carried me through so many fractured moments. I realised I could act without waiting for permission, that my voice mattered, and that I was capable of creating meaning even amidst uncertainty. The digital noise that had consumed me – messages, forums, endless threads of hope and heartbreak – was replaced by reflection, by a calm that I hadn't felt in years. My chest no longer hammered with frantic urgency; it beat steady, like a blacksmith at the forge, each strike measured, purposeful.

The landscape of egg donation in Australia was jagged and rocky, the need urgent, the lists lengthening by the day. I resolved to start a public conversation, to shine a light on this hidden world – for those isolated and seeking support, for anyone who could lend a hand, and for all those whose hope had yet to find its path. And in doing so, I found a clarity I had never known; a sense of self not defined by chaos or fear, but by purpose, courage, and a quiet determination to make a difference.

I reached out to find others whose vision matched mine.

Faith was a blonde bombshell with a larger-than-life personality. She was the poster girl for egg donation in Australia; a visionary whose ideas seemed ahead of their time. Soon, we were talking daily. She no longer donated her eggs but remained devoted to helping others. Vibrant, with an infectious laugh and a devilish sense of humour, she lit up every conversation. I loved that about her.

I then reached out to a woman named Christina, whose donation blog I had followed for a year. She was intelligent, organised, articulate, and deeply compassionate. Her motivation was personal – she had watched a family member struggle with infertility, and though she herself didn't need an egg donor, she wanted to support someone who did. When she saw egg donor ads in the newspaper go unanswered for six months, she thought: if I can't help my own, perhaps I can help someone else. Successful in her career, she understood that life was about more than money or achievement; she wanted to be part of something greater. Matter of fact and quick-witted, Christina carried a humour that made her presence effervescent, lifting everyone around her. After discussing our idea, she was in.

The three of us set to work creating an organisation together. Though very different women, each bringing unique skills, we balanced each other beautifully – ready and willing to build something meaningful together.

In May 2011, Egg Donation Australia was born. At times, I wondered what on earth we were thinking – bumping our own posts, trying to spark engagement, navigating the pitfalls of media attention, while my own self-doubt screamed in the background.

But soon, our little bird found its wings and flew, our small village blossoming into a thriving community. Faith and I became close, our conversations stretching for hours. She was electric, magical, like watching fireworks explode frame by frame in slow motion. She radiated light, and I was drawn to her energy.

When we talked, our words weaved between the coldest shadows and the purest morning light. She confided that she had been unwell, had a tumour, yet reduced the weight of her illness to a minor ailment. Treatment was underway, she said, and she would be fine. She brushed aside any notion of self-pity or loathing. Faith was a clash of opposites – equally terrified and defiant, a quiet storm contained within.

There was something in her voice, a defiance like a distant star refusing to burn out quietly. Sometimes, we simply sat in silence, searching for words we had left unspoken.

Through this journey, alongside finding purpose, I discovered friendships I might never have encountered anywhere else. With these people, I belonged. I found a sense of purpose that unfurled like spring blossoms, soft and inevitable. In them, I had found a home.

Faith's voice teased down the line, soft and amused. 'You'll never believe what I did today.'

I smiled instinctively. 'That's usually true.'

She chuckled. 'I was walking past this tiny, run-down bookstore – the kind with faded signs and crooked windows – and something just pulled me in. You know I hate clutter, but this place was like stepping into someone's memory. Dust motes everywhere, piles of books like little cities.'

'Sounds like your version of hell,' I said.

'I know! But listen… I found this old poetry collection, hand-bound, no author name, no date. Just titled *Things That Wait*. Isn't that the most haunting title?'

I made a soft sound of agreement.

She hummed thoughtfully. 'I sat there in this cracked leather chair with stuffing coming out of the seams, reading these poems that felt like the writer had folded their life into stanzas and left it for a stranger to discover. And I just started crying. Right there in front of the old shopkeeper who probably thought I was having a breakdown.'

'Were you?'

'Maybe a small one. But the good kind. A beautiful one. You

know, when you remember parts of yourself you forgot existed.'

She paused. Her voice softened, as if something inside her had exhaled.

'I think I've been so focused on surviving that I forgot how to simply… feel things. Without fear.'

A silence settled between us, gentle and full. I could picture her – bathed in quiet sunlight, surrounded by words not her own, and yet somehow more herself than ever. Some part of me ached with knowing. There is something sacred about watching someone rediscover themselves.

'I guess today reminded me that there's still wonder out there,' she said. 'Even for people like me. People who've lived too close to endings.'

She breathed in, then added lightly, 'Anyway. Enough of that emotional drivel. Otherwise, I'll have to start charging you for therapy.'

I laughed. 'You're impossible.'

She chuckled too, and it was such a refreshing sound – like rain after a long dry spell.

Hearing her laugh was always a kind of healing. Our conversations weren't just diversions; they were little lifelines, strung between grief and grace. Despite everything, Faith had a way of seeing the light. She could still thread humour through sorrow like a silver seam.

I asked about her health, even though I already knew. Her silences often said more than her words, but I needed to ask. I needed to hear her voice dance through the dark, just a little longer.

She deflected, as always, cloaking the truth in her signature wit. When we met in person, she wore her illness like an inside joke – visible only to those who looked too long. She still looked heartbreakingly radiant – golden hair, doll-like features, a million-watt smile. It was cruel, how beauty could coexist so effortlessly with suffering.

'How are you doing though?' I asked, smiling into the silence.

'I'm doing what you do,' she replied, her voice teasing. 'Deflecting with humour and not facing things for a while.'

'Touché.'

She sighed then, the kind of sigh that holds more than fatigue – it held resignation, bravery, and something like peace.

'It's not going brilliantly. The tumour was too dangerous to remove. They injected ethanol to kill it, but it's stubborn, still in my liver. No other surgical options – they're too risky. So now, the ritual of daily painkillers. I wear morphine patches and pretend they're tattoos because I'm too chicken to get one. Hubby's in shock, so I take advantage. Arms around him, I hug, and maybe… reach into his pocket for his wallet.'

I chuckled. 'Why not?'

Then she leaned into something darker, quieter, yet still laced with her dry humour.

'If the worst happens, I've decided to hold an organ garage sale. I ticked all the boxes for organ donation – except for my eyes. Not that anyone asks about fat arses or protruding bellies!'

She let out a mock dramatic sigh.

I laughed – half in amusement, half in awe. How did she manage it? To find laughter even at the edge of the unthinkable.

I couldn't imagine her position. I couldn't walk it with her. But in that moment, I could at least sit beside her, word by word.

'And you? How are things with you? You've had a rough time lately.'

I smiled, though it felt fragile. 'No, not like you. Your news makes my troubles look like a walk in the park. Things with Lucas have been better. I'm starting to wonder if he's finally coming around.'

'So good to hear. Life has a way of working out like it's supposed to. I'm here for you too. It's you and me versus the world, sister.'

Her voice had something in it then – fierce, familiar, a kind of unspoken promise.

'Count me in,' I said.

7

Later that year, Lucas asked me to marry him. He had proposed after ten years together, and I'd said yes.

After nearly a decade together, saying yes felt almost fated, as if time itself had been carrying me forward. I was optimistic – I saw a period of good and reassured myself that marriage might be the turning point for us. That a ring, a vow, the promise of permanence would make him safe, would make *me* safe. I told myself marriage could mend what was behind us, could finally give me the security I craved. Saying yes carried all those old echoes, yet still, I stepped into it willingly, letting optimism guide me, daring to believe that love could finally feel whole, unburdened by fear, and free of the need to shrink to survive.

Before the big day, my friends threw me a hen's night. I didn't know it then, but I was about to meet another of the great loves of my life: my best friend, Sarah. The evening began early, an undercurrent of excitement in the air. The women gathered around white linen tables set with bottomless champagne and delicate high tea platters. Hours in, the guests' conversations had become a murmur of laughter, flushed cheeks, and messy elegance. A few faces I'd only known online, yet they had come to celebrate with me in person – bold enough to step into the unknown, into our rowdy, wine-laced celebration.

'Hi, Mel,' a voice called from behind me.

'Hi!' I said, wrapping her in a hug before I realised who she was. When I pulled back, those yellow-green cat eyes met mine, a Cheshire-cat smile playing at her lips – Sarah. We had been messaging for months, our humour and spirit entwined across screens, and now, in the living glow of the party, she was real. We even shared a birthday, which felt like a lucky omen.

'Thanks for inviting me!' she laughed, and it felt like the start of something inevitable.

'Hope we don't scare you with our drunken naughtiness,' I teased.

'Scare me? This is perfect. Pleasantries are done and dusted,' she replied, her words sharp and warm, like sunlight through glass.

The table erupted again.

'Oh my god. What is that?'

Someone brandished a bright pink vibrator from the gift basket, and laughter and cheers rose from the group, full-bodied and free. Lingerie, novelties, the ridiculous and the risqué – chaos reigned, and I laughed in gleeful surrender as the girls rifled through it.

Later, hair loose, heels abandoned, we stumbled, laughing, back to the rented apartment, wine in hand, voices intertwining with the dim streetlights and quiet sounds of the coastal neighbourhood. Hours passed unnoticed. The first light of dawn spilled over the blinds, soft and forgiving. It had been a night alive with mischief, discovery, and the unmistakable spark of a friendship that would last a lifetime.

The long-awaited wedding day dawned, pale light spilling through the curtains, illuminating the room with a sense of quiet anticipation. I stood before the mirror, gazing at my dress and the bouquet of delicate flowers, fingertips brushing the petals as if tracing the shape of the future it might hold. The house hummed with soft, purposeful movement — friends and family readying themselves for the day ahead.

Marrying Lucas was the culmination of nearly a decade together, our lives intertwined through two daughters who had already taught me so much about love, patience, and endurance. Today was for them as much as it was for us — a chance to mark continuity, to give shape to the family we had built, despite the flaws and fractures threading through it. I knew the cracks in our foundation, the shadows that lingered, yet I let the morning light fill the room, willing myself to see possibility.

Outside, the gardens were alive with greenery and flowers, dew catching the morning sun, a reminder that life moved forward, whether we were ready or not. I carried hope lightly, differently than before — less a shield against fear, more a fragile compass pointing toward possibility. I loved him, I loved our girls, and I allowed myself to believe that, at least for today, joy could exist alongside the uncertainty, that beauty could coexist with imperfection.

As I prepared to walk down the aisle, the venue beckoned with its picturesque charm. Nestled lakeside, adorned with grand architecture with a fusion of French and Italian influences, it served as the idyllic backdrop for our vows. Neutral hues mingled with vibrant blooms, creating a scene straight out of a fairytale.

Admiring the cobblestone driveway lined by crimson maples, I paused to absorb the beauty surrounding me. Beside me stood Lucas, his gaze filled with intensity and love, sparking a hope for the future. With our children by our side, we exchanged vows beneath the azure sky, surrounded by loved ones and celebrating a new chapter of our shared history.

As the night went on, and as the final notes of the last dance faded into the night, we walked out hand in hand, mingling beneath the stars. We eased back into the rhythm of everyday life; there was no honeymoon or fuss. There was just he and I and the family we had already made, and yet, somehow, we felt different now. I had hope, the unwavering belief in the possibility of better days, and the heartbeat of resilience, reminding us that, despite the challenges we had faced, there was always reason to believe in a better future.

There are few people we are instantly drawn to as though we have known each other all our lives.

When I first chatted to Tereasa just days before my wedding, she was that person. Across continents and oceans and parallel lives, we connected online. I may never have spoken to her should we have met in passing in a restaurant, library, or wine bar, but this is the splendour of fate, forging connections we might not have made for ourselves.

Tereasa was hard to miss. She wore bright scarves, bold prints, and flowing fabrics that mirrored the energy and colour inside her. There was something alive about her — something that drew people in, made them want to listen and stay. Her mind overflowed with ideas and stories, and she shared them generously, like someone scattering seeds wherever she went. She was a writer, an artist, someone who turned her thoughts into words that felt both delicate and true. And yet, for all her colour and warmth, there was a quiet part of her that longed for something deeply human and achingly simple: to be a mother. She was like a splash of brightness in a world that often felt grey – a reminder that even the most vibrant people can carry an unspoken ache beneath the surface.

It started with honest truths. 'I've been researching donor options since January. I contacted overseas clinics, and they sent profiles of their donors. Initially, I thought if I can't have my genetics, I might as well trade up. But then I read the profiles, which felt impersonal and almost dirty, like I was shopping for my child's genetics in a catalogue of strangers. That bothered me. So, I started searching for other options. I found myself sitting one night in my Hong Kong apartment, staring out at the bright lights of the big city, feeling alone, when I found EDA. My searches brought me here to a safe space, where I felt welcomed and understood. I hope to interact with you, learn from you, and share with you on our journeys.'

Her words were candid, which was refreshing in a world of people who told you what they believed you wanted to hear, anything it took to find a donor. Being commodified or catalogued by physical features, critiqued by insensitive strangers can be tough when the process isn't purely transactional.

Although I understood why those needing a donor might want a donor with similar physical characteristics, I liked the way she spoke earnestly, baring her soul, and I admired her tenacity.

She was thirty-seven. She and her husband, Charles, lived in Hong Kong city. He was Kenyan, and she was Australian. He worked as an investment banker, and she was a corporate communicator. He ran marathons over mountains; she wrote and painted Chinese ink paintings. Nine years before, they had first met in a Japanese nightclub. Tokyo had amazing nightlife, the music scene was a veritable melting pot full of people from the Caribbean, Latin America, Russia, and Australia.

When I wrote her an email, I typed tentatively, putting great thought into the message. Her responses were reflective and beautifully complex, like her forum posts. My replies were considered and purposeful, matching her energy, even though my life at that time was busy and demanding.

I wanted to get to the essence of who she was, never one for small talk. She'd lived a full life; educated, worldly, and well-travelled. We talked about our love of words and the arts, relationships, and families. She lived a unique life, making no apologies for fitting all the living possible into her one vibrant life. What she hadn't experienced, and the thing she wanted most, was motherhood. It wasn't as though they hadn't tried. Still young, she assumed it would come quickly when the time was right.

Tereasa had become pregnant twice; each time, her hope turning to grief as she picked up the pieces, unsure what had gone wrong. She confided about a loss at thirteen weeks; the memory of holding a tiny translucent foetus in her hands as she wept. It was the size of her thumb. She'd given birth to a baby that would never be. Overwhelmed, she never wanted to face such pain ever again. It was too unreal a concept for me to comprehend, a scene I couldn't create because I had never been there.

I gently broached her need for a donor. What did she want from a donor? How would the donation work with her living in Hong Kong and her donor being Australian? She replied that she was hoping anyone willing to donate would travel to Thailand. Tereasa had a rare blood clotting disorder that doctors had struggled to diagnose accurately.

Hospitalised with blood clots, she managed the risk with medication and check-ups, otherwise living a normal life. Her specialists suggested her challenges with pregnancy were related to egg quality issue and a low egg reserve. With that in mind, she began the search for a donor. Long flights might cause deep vein thrombosis, creating clots that could be dangerous – even fatal – so she needed to limit air travel. Thailand was a short flight away, and Hong Kong's laws did not allow donation. Clinics in Thailand were known for fertility treatments such as IVF egg and surrogacy arrangements. Being put under a general anaesthetic in a non-English-speaking country was not something appealing to many people.

Faith loved the idea. 'Thailand is bloody amazing. They have great facilities. I've donated there a couple of times. It's so easy. Their medical technology is of a high standard. Plus, the shopping and the food. You'll love it.'

She made good points. My parents lived in Thailand for several years, the country like a second home. I could see them while I was there.

Our connection blossomed further via video call. She was a vision, with her fair hair framing porcelain skin and cheeks like cherry blossoms. She wore vintage-inspired dresses, each a mosaic of vibrant hues, complemented by eye-catching decorative jewellery.

She was driven, creative, passionate, and always thinking. Our conversations continued for hours as we drank tea from our lounge rooms on different sides of the world and discussed the possibilities of the universe. The connection between us deepened, enriched by the exchange of profound ideas.

My daughters were drawn to the woman on the screen. With eager anticipation, they leaned in towards the laptop as she read stories and displayed her collection of books. Ava, despite her tender age of four and still grappling with speech, blossomed around Tereasa.

I soon discovered that Ava had been making secret video calls to talk to her while I studied, with Tereasa giving her a tour of her apartment and refrigerator. When she told me what had happened, I was mortified. Tereasa embraced the situation with humour and grace. Her acceptance and willingness to engage with Ava's escapades underscored her genuine affection.

Tereasa's fondness for my daughters served as a constant reminder of my blessings. Lily, with her spirited intellect, resembled midnight blue – deep and resolute. In contrast, Ava was daffodil yellow, embodying a gentle, colourful spirit, thriving in her own vibrant world. Raised with differing degrees of hands-on parenting, they each flourished in their unique ways.

The joyous news of previous recipients conceiving twins fuelled our hope for Tereasa's journey. As the days passed, the pieces of our plan fell into place. The initial brainstorming sessions, filled with enthusiasm and boundless ideas, gradually gave way to focused action. With each conversation, each decision made, our collective determination grew stronger, propelling us forward with unwavering resolve. Her dream had become my dream also. I was invested.

'Geez!' Faith moaned. 'My luck has got to turn around soon. . . but small blessings, right? We received the news that I'm off to Thailand for surgery. We are not sure when yet. I'd rather be getting a boob job than liver surgery, but hey, what can you do? It could be done in Australia, but surgeons are so protective of their stats, and the fact it is so high-risk that they won't do it pisses me off no end. But that's life, right?'

I wrinkled my nose.

'Yeah, not much of a silver lining, but at least it's something. It's what you were wanting, right?' The bittersweet news a Thai hospital would operate while Australian surgeons had refused was fresh in our minds. While it was hope, the news steered us into 'what if' territory. It might give her life back, but there was the possibility things could go wrong, and Faith might not make it home.

'I think about my life. I haven't finished living yet. I'm forty-two,' she said. 'I'm far too young to be thinking about things like writing wills and picking my funeral music. I'm sitting in an office, slaving away on my days off, wasting my life, and for what? I could be doing so many other things!' she said stubbornly.

'Sometimes I feel selfish. I have a child and have loved a grandchild. I have been to Paris, have married a good man, and am torturing the crap out of the one I married first!' She laughed mischievously, continuing, 'But I've made my mark on this life, and to think that's maybe three or four things many others haven't done or experienced. I have parents whom I love and who are still in love with each other, great friends, a wonderful EDA family here, and a great DVD and CD collection, so why can't I be grateful and accepting?'

'Is it ever that easy? When you have so much happiness, why would you not want to live as much life as possible? It's easy to take life for granted, not to realise its value until it's gone or is slipping from our fingers. When faced with losing something, wanting to live as long as possible is human. I feel like that often, too. I wake up, rush to get the kids dressed, go to work, bathe, have dinner, and bed, then do it all again. Rinse, repeat. Sometimes I wonder what for. We make ends meet; sometimes it feels like daycare raises my kids.

'I tell myself… Mel, you are twenty-nine years old. You have a husband and children and responsibilities. Get up, go to work and keep doing it. That is what adults do, and it's what you have to look forward to every day for the next thirty years. Suck it up! But isn't life so much more than that?! I wonder what kind of life we would live if we lived like each day was our last.'

'I certainly wouldn't be stuck in that office,' she snorted.

'Faith, you have spent your life serving others, almost to a point where it's part of your identity. Maybe you should focus on yourself, live your dreams, and find joy again?' I prodded gently. 'I remember you telling me you had organised insurance for if you didn't make it and wrote letters to those you love, on the chance you didn't come home. You told me about your bucket list, the one we all have on the shelf if we have forever to start. Not a bucket list for dying, but a bucket list for living. Tell me what's on your list?'

Faith laughed softly. 'Well, in case they call out my name to board the escalator to Heaven, I guess I won't want to be pondering the things I wish I'd have done before leaving,' she said.

'Here's my list,' she began. 'I would tell my ex-husband he traded down with his second wife. I think he secretly knows anyway,' she joked.

'Of course he does!' I insisted with a laugh.

'I'd have gotten a tattoo that rocks. I'd go back to Paris and buy a dress, just so I can say, "This is my Paris dress." I would remove all the photos on social media taken of me in the last five years – I look like I founded the Ferguson Plarre's Bakery Fan Club.' She snorted. 'And I would wear more low-cut tops! The girls have had me under house arrest with every outfit I wear. I might as well be Amish.'

'Funny. What else?' I prompted.

'I'd have gone back to the Sydney Mardi Gras. So many colours to wear while dancing around in a pair of boots and grinding against men who look at my face and not my chest takes me back ten years!' she replied, her voice brimming with amusement.

'New York for Christmas, skydiving, and I would have learned how to play the tambourine. All cool chicks in the cartoons play one; think Daphne on Scooby Doo. That's the only one I can think of, but it still sounds good.'

'Okay,' I replied. 'So, where do we start?'

'Maybe I'll call my ex first. Then I'm going to go shopping for a low-cut, sparkly number. The kind people at Visa and MasterCard have said, "Go forth and spend; don't worry about the interest rate" – so I will.'

'Yeah. You have fun with that,' I joked.

'I'm off to Sydney to meet the girls. Wish you could come.'

'Next time, I'm there.'

'You better be.'

8

On a beautiful Sunday morning in Sydney's North Shore, I sat admiring the view from a charming café perched above the glistening indigo sea. The morning sun illuminated the golden sand, casting a radiant glow upon it while children sat in the sand, building sandcastles beyond the reach of the waterline.

Around the weathered tables, a group of women sat, laughter and conversations flowing effortlessly – they were all the women I'd donated eggs to in the past four years. Time seemed to stand still in this sanctuary of togetherness, where worries melted away, and hearts found safety in the company of kindred spirits. In these moments, surrounded by friends, the world felt alive with possibility, and the simple act of sitting, talking, and laughing was easy and joyous.

The women I had chosen to donate to, I loved differently. Jaye was witty and intelligent, and I fell in love with how she wrote. Her authenticity. Trudi could laugh infectiously through the toughest of times, this was the way she lived life. Mel was kind, gentle, and positive. Julie was smart and boldly honest with a great sense of humour. Lou was gentle and considerate. Dee loved life and being around her brought you alive. Kim was a firecracker; strong and fierce. There was a strength, a camaraderie, a shared, quiet understanding.

They were all different seasons, a warm blanket in the cold winter, a birdsong in the spring, autumn leaves in warm tones, setting the forests aglow with their fiery intensity and summer skies, a masterpiece of their own, painted with strokes of cerulean blue. I would choose them over and over again.

Brought together by shared hope; the goals of becoming a mother or wanting to help someone become a mother. Following our meal, we strolled along the beachside lanes to the residence of one of the women, where Christina and I had been staying.

I received a message from Tereasa. 'I am freaking out like you would not believe. I did two home pregnancy tests. Two! My period was a bit late, and I thought no big deal, right? So, just for the hell of it, I went down to the chemist and got a cheap home pregnancy test. Positive. I had a minor freak out, turned around and went back out the door and to the chemist again. Then I got an expensive test. I came back and tested. Positive! I am in shock. Can it be true? Surely not. My God. . . I'm pregnant, and I don't have a clue what to do!'

I could sense her panic, written there beneath each line in places I knew weren't empty, like the blank spaces between stanzas in poetry, but she was not ready to be that vulnerable, she was afraid to jinx it. Unwritten and unspoken ghosts tell their own story.

To someone who had already suffered heartbreaking losses, the news brought anxiety and uncertainty. Every pregnancy she had been given had been stolen away. Her husband, Charles, was at work, and she needed someone to talk to.

Her specialist believed she had previously miscarried due to a blood clotting disorder, putting her on blood plasma infusion treatment, hoping it might help her pregnancy to continue. It was a gamble. At thousands of dollars for each treatment, it was a choice made in desperation. When I returned home to Queensland from Sydney, she was five weeks pregnant, with another specialist appointment two days later.

Her results came in, bittersweet.

'The news isn't good. Only a small increase – I'm not what I'd call "pregnant" yet. More than anything else, I've got the comfort of your support. I give myself over to this process and am in the hands of creation. Today, I'm just going to rest, relax, and enjoy. No high tension, no drama – unless it's on TV – no poking medical procedures, and no surprises. I've had enough for one week. What will be will be. So, the kettle's on. Anyone for a cuppa? I'm now in an eight-day wait, and everything will be roses, kittens, flowers, and fabulous classic novels.'

She threw an online tea party; up went the invitation, and her online thread lit up with replies and images of elaborate hats, found on the far-reaching corners of internet fashion pages.

Fabulous locations, decadent food and 1920s movie starlets with elegance and style, we picked up our virtual teacups and ball gowns and stayed with her for a while. Although we were thousands of miles apart, gathered in lounge rooms and offices across Australia, we were beside her. I knew the odds. The shitty statistics. But hope shone brighter. She held on, asking for a miracle. She chose joy. Through doubt, she saw beauty and magic in life. I'd never admired her as I did at that moment.

She created me a virtual golden birdcage hat with giant feathers, spilling over with wildflowers. We shared our bucket lists of exotic locations: Canada's green mountainous lakes, the blue lagoons of tropical Bora Bora, an underwater restaurant and hotel, a ski chalet in southern France, and a villa in the Cook Islands. It was a wild and wonderful distraction. Tereasa let go, trusting the universe and accepting whatever would come. Finally, the day of the scan came.

'I'm pregnant with twins. It's my wildest dream! They're alive, but quite small. One's heart is beating quite slowly. It means it's high-risk. If one goes, it usually means they both go. So, it's great they're alive, but we're a long way from celebrating yet. So, the tea party continues. I am officially pregnant. I'm still reaching for them, asking them to stay with me, and telling them how much I love them. They're still tiny little beans and will have to fight hard to make it into this world. I hope they've got a whole lot of fight in them.'

She appeared optimistic but called to talk as I drove home from work. I pulled to the shoulder of the road, giving her my full attention.

'I'm officially pregnant, Mel, but I'm terrified.'

I offered encouraging words. Not because I felt them, but because she needed them. Deep down, I thought many things I didn't dare say aloud. The miscarriage rate was high, but there were always the exceptions.

Days later, we were up late, video calling. Tereasa looked tired, her eyes sullen and lost. She obviously had much on her mind. She broke down.

'Mel, I know this isn't good. I've lost so many babies now. My body is broken. Maybe Charles is right about looking into other options. I'm terrified this might not ever happen for us. I'm in so much pain. I'm sad and beyond tired. Some days, I wish the world would swallow me up.' Her cheeks were flushed, and her eyes spilled over with tears.

'Tereasa, you're not alone in this. If you can't carry these babies I'll carry one for you. You WILL be a mum, whatever happens.'

She looked at me in silence, slowly nodding, but also conflicted. 'Thank you for being here for me, Mel.'

Realising the time, we said goodnight. We both needed sleep and hoped tomorrow's scan would deliver good news.

'There are no heartbeats, and the sacs have turned into big, dark balls. It's all over, Mel. I felt like the room was crashing down around me, and I had to get out of there.'

I could hear the heartache in her voice as she fought to get the words out.

'Oh, honey, I'm so sorry.'

We had considered this news likely, but the bad news was still devastating. She updated her online diary: 'Tears are streaming down my face as I write this. But I have to say I have enjoyed this short time of feeling what it is like to be pregnant again. I like the feeling of it. My body feels still, alive, and so full of promise. It would have been such a dream to have beautiful little twins, but it is indeed almost too beautiful. Too incredible to be true. And it is no longer valid. There were no longer any heartbeats.

'I've got to hop to it about getting on a plane to Australia before I start to miscarry. I'd prefer not to go through it naturally. It was painful the first time, and I still so clearly remember holding my little boy, no larger than my thumb, in my hands. I don't want to face that again. I'm broken.

'There's much to consider regarding the next steps. For now, though, I want to crawl into a tight ball and cry. I know there is a future, and I will come back to you feeling brighter on another day.

I won't stay in this space long or stick here feeling sad. But right this minute, it is the absolute pits.'

Tears fell for her as I curled into the corner of my lounge. I video called and saw her face on my screen, downcast. She had decided to fly back to Australia to seek medical advice. With family in Sydney, she would be in good hands.

In the days following and as she left Hong Kong, I let her be. After her procedure and leaving the hospital, she retreated to a quiet beach to think, to breathe, to grieve. Finally, she came up for air, writing an update.

'I don't mind the rain. Or the cold. I'm wrapping myself in the grey sky, the rain like tears, in big blankets and staring at the sea. It's appropriate and a final kind apology from Mother Nature that she sends me gentle rain and purple storms instead of the harsh sun for frolicking. This recovery weather will last a week. I'm impressed with nature. By the end of the week, I might be inclined to forgive her and even be prepared for a frolic. I'm not putting a timeline on it nor attaching my recovery to the weather. I'm just saying. . . I might have thawed a bit towards her then. She's not in the gold-star book today, but enough of this rainy apologising, and if she sends me some humpback whales, I'll reconsider our relationship.'

When she finally called, it was a relief to hear her voice.

'How are you?' I asked gently.

'I'm okay. I feel strangely at peace. I'm still a little sad.'

'That's understandable,' I answered. 'If there's anything I can do, I'm here.'

I let her lead the conversation as she unpacked her thoughts. I'd had dozens of my own swirling for days but remained quiet. Part of me wanted to move in and sweep her up and make everything okay again. I'd seen the fight in her, and I wanted to watch her rise, surge ahead and keep going, but grief keeps its own time.

She would let me know when she was ready. It came sooner than expected. She started the conversations right there and then.

'I can't handle drowning in grief and doing nothing. I need something positive to focus on. Although this is over, the dream remains.'

We had discussed options briefly when she was in Hong Kong, but it was never the right time to talk about it seriously. And now, there were more questions than answers; questions this pregnancy brought to the surface. She had come to EDA to find an egg donor but had fallen pregnant with her egg. Would she still need a donor? What about her ability to carry?

Charles had spoken about getting a surrogate, unable to bear watching her miscarry, and fearing a complication might leave him without a wife and a child. The pregnancy loss raised more questions, and no one had answers.

'When you are up for it, I want you to come and see Dr Ong. He's a miscarriage specialist. I trust him. If anyone can help you, he can,' I told her.

'Hmmm, that's a good idea. Maybe we could see another doctor on the same day?' she replied. 'It might give us different opinions. I'll book a flight and come up.'

I hugged her when she arrived at the airport gate. We were meeting for the first time, yet she felt as familiar as an old friend. As we drove home, we talked about what the future held. Hope was in her voice, sparks of life smouldering in the ashes, ready to catch fire.

We sat down in a little café, drinking tea while shoppers

bustled around us. Tereasa looked uncomfortable. Pulling her seat back, she lifted her knee, rubbing the back of her leg.

She frowned. 'My leg feels sore. I've felt like this before. I'm unsure if I'm overthinking it.'

I studied her pained expression. 'You've been on a long flight. Maybe you should get it checked out.'

We drove to the emergency department of our local hospital, and she was admitted immediately.

'So, this is where you work?' Tereasa asked, looking around. 'It looks exciting. Is it like Grey's Anatomy? There are plenty of hot doctors,' she joked, lightening the mood. Of course she was joking at a time like this. For several hours, we entertained ourselves as doctors and nurses came in and out of the room. A scan revealed a fifteen-centimetre blood clot in her groin.

'I'm glad you came in today.' The young doctor looked at her with a thoughtful expression as he fiddled with his clipboard. 'We will need you to see a haematologist and alter your medication to break up that blood clot.'

The hospital gave scripts and discharged her. We arrived home that night with even more to consider. What had caused this? The answer soon became apparent.

We sat across from Dr Ong in his office the following day as he studied her files. 'Did you notice that each of your pregnancies has been followed by a substantial blood clot, regardless of the length of gestation? There is a risk these clots could break and kill you. You should see a haematologist, and it's my opinion that you need to consider finding a surrogate, and you should not attempt to get pregnant again. You need to look after your health.' He spoke gently but with a serious tone. He handed her a business card for a haematologist. 'I can call and ask him to fit you in ASAP.'

We saw the haematologist just hours later and he confirmed Dr Ong's prognosis.

Looking at her gravely, he said, 'You should not only stop trying to get pregnant, but you should take active measures to make sure there are no accidents. I would highly recommend you avoid fertility treatments and consider the paths of adoption or surrogacy. The risk is far too high. It's life-threatening. If you progressed further in your pregnancies, it may have resulted in your death. I'm sorry to deliver this news.'

The final fertility specialist agreed with the others. Tereasa appeared calm as she listened, almost relieved to have an answer. The tension around her seemed to ease, as though a heavy weight had been lifted. I could see the fear, the longing, and the grief all at once, and it made my chest ache.

Later, when I was alone with my thoughts, I faced my own reckoning. I knew what it would mean to carry another person's child: the physical strain, the exhaustion, the vulnerability, the months of uncertainty and medical oversight. I understood there were real risks, that my body could be tested in ways I had never imagined. And yet, each risk was met with a quiet insistence in my heart.

I thought of Tereasa – of her hope, of the life she longed to hold, of the joy she deserved. I thought of the possibility of giving her something she could not have on her own, and it was almost unbearable not to act. Despite the weight of danger, despite knowing I could face hardships no one could predict, I felt a certainty I could not ignore.

We had many conversations following those appointments. Together, we made some big decisions.

I would carry her baby.

She shared an update with friends on the Egg Donation Australia portal: 'Luckily, I am blessed to have Mel's support (and much more) on our parenthood quest. She has generously offered to be a surrogate and carry Charles' and my future beautiful baby into the world. Can you believe it? I am so happy about this. It is mind-blowing. One of the dark days, when the HCG wasn't rising correctly and my body was tired, we chatted on Skype. I told her I wanted the world to swallow me up. She paused briefly and wrote, "Tereasa, if you can't carry these babies, I will carry one for you."

'For the first, and I think the only time in my life, I was speechless. I sat back on the sofa, and tears streamed down my face. I think it took me a long time to write back. I think I said, "Thank you." It's going to be a long journey.

'We have yet to nail down the details and get a timeline. We know it will either happen this year or next year. Regarding the following steps: I will prepare to do my egg cycle this year. It might be an abject failure; it might not. Either way, I cannot go through my life wondering, "What if?"

'After I cycle, we will know if I need an egg donor to knock that beautiful lady Mel up! I can't wait until I see her pregnant, and I can't wait until I know I have a baby on the way. This is the most exciting project I have ever worked on. I am so grateful to Mel and you all, as it is through this community I feel capable of taking on such a significant journey. As always, I will keep you all posted on our progress. In the meantime, I expect everyone who sees Mel to hug her for me! It's incredible to think her friendship will change my life forever. It's already changed my life because I do have a life with hope in it.'

With that, we began a new journey. Tereasa returned home to Hong Kong but was never far from my thoughts.

I entered the medical assessment ward of the hospital right before changeover time. There were teams of doctors in pressed chinos and expensive Italian leather shoes in circles around mobile workstations. The nurses were beginning their handovers before they left for the day.

There, I met Winston, a man with dementia in his early seventies. He paced the sterile halls like a caged lion, back and forth, end to end, his limbs frail but his movement feverish. His skin drooped, age eroding his muscle mass, his mind unaware. Winston had been a marathon runner in his younger days, his body in perpetual motion, but his memory gone.

Signs of a lost era still lingered as he paced the linear corridors rhythmically. A nurse followed him, handing him a clear cup containing pills. He collected them from her, not missing a beat. With the tilt of his head and a chaser of water, they were gone. He threw the discarded vessels over his shoulder as he powered on, the cups bouncing across the floor. She scooped them up without hesitation and tossed them in a nearby bin.

In the second room was a young girl new to the ward. She had sad eyes and wore an oversized blue cardigan over her petite frame. Her skin was ivory but flushed with red. She picked at her nails, her left arm resting in a support sling. Her left eye was sunken, brushed with crimson and lavender bruising on her eyelid and under her socket. That would be a shiner tomorrow.

Several patients in the surrounding rooms had friends visiting or relatives stroking their hair and holding their hands. But the girl in blue was alone, cradling her knees to her chest, trying her best to look small and invisible.

'Is she okay?' I asked the nurse making notes outside.

'She's here, that's something, I suppose,' the nurse responded dryly. 'Her name is Jennifer. Twenty-eight years old and beat up by the boyfriend. Her notes suggest she's a frequent flyer. Fractured lower ulna and bruising to the nose and left eye socket. MRI scan clear. We are just waiting for the social worker to see her.'

Taking a heated blanket from the warmer, I approached her bedside, introduced myself, and offered her the blanket. She accepted it with a grateful half-smile. Her eyes teared up, and I patted her shoulder gently as the social worker arrived. Offering a reassuring smile as I left, my mind didn't leave her side for the rest of the night.

There was something about her that had crept too close and right up into my comfort zone. My world was overlapped with hers, prompting comparisons to my life and relationship, while I presented myself with justifications for our differences. I could not forget the darkness, the grief. The way that look used to feel. I grieved for both of us. I thought of Tereasa and how her future counted on me keeping my shit together.

'Thank you for waiting. How can I help you today?' The lawyer closed the door and sat on his leather office chair, leaning over his desk, and adjusting his tie. I reached into my bag for an envelope of paperwork and slid it across the glass desktop to him. 'My name is Melissa. I've got a surrogacy agreement. I need legal advice.'

He didn't hide his surprise; he looked down at the papers he'd retrieved from the envelope and across at me with curiosity. Thumbing through the pages silently, he stroked his beard. We'd researched the process and begun taking steps to make surrogacy a reality. I understood what we were doing. Finally, he looked up.

'You know how this works?'

I nodded.

'Yes, I've researched this in detail. I know what I'm doing. Surrogacy in Australia is altruistic. Legally, I'm giving birth to a child, and my name will be on the birth certificate, although the child will be in their care. We then do a parenting order in the courts, and the child is transferred legally to the intended parents.'

He smiled, seeming satisfied. He rattled off a few standard further statements of law before handing the papers back to me. I took the pen and signed on the dotted lines. He witnessed and stamped the paperwork before returning it to the yellow envelope.

'Thank you.' I gathered up my bag, ready to leave.

'One more question,' he asked.

'Of course.'

'How much do they pay you?'

My confusion must have been evident.

'They don't pay me. Tereasa is my friend.'

He paused, taking in my answer before firmly shaking my hand. He opened the office door, ushering me out.

As I reached for my purse, he shook his head. 'No, it's taken care of. Look after yourself.'

'Thank you.' I smiled gratefully. Wow. It had gone well; the positive responses received from strangers had been encouraging.

The day before, we had attended counselling. Tereasa, our husbands, and I participated in the session in a busy office building in Brisbane. The chairs had been spread around the room in a half circle, the room, with large shelves from floor to ceiling, stacked with textbooks.

A small box of toys and children's drawings was in the corner above the hardwood desk. The view from the office window was of surrounding roofs and balconies lined with potted chrysanthemums and succulents.

The counsellor, a tall, thin man with white, wiry curls, appeared, his grin as wild as his hair. He introduced himself. I had met him several times before during egg donation counselling sessions and had grown used to his unorthodox style. What followed was over three hours of questions and pointed comments.

He chuckled to himself as he called me a 'prize stud'. I could only laugh and shake my head as Tereasa looked on wide-eyed. Explaining how surrogacy worked, he asked questions about possible scenarios that could occur during a surrogacy journey.

What would we do if something was wrong with the baby? Would we terminate? If either couple separated, how would we cope? What if my life was at risk during pregnancy? What if our relationship broke down? What if Tereasa or Charles died, or both? Who would care for the baby? Did we have any expectations? Concerns? How did we picture the birth? The list of questions was long.

Lucas and I left the room while he spoke to Tereasa and Charles and sat down to complete psychometric tests. Later, we switched places. The counsellor had questions.

'Why do you want to do this for Tereasa and Charles?' he asked.

For me, the answer was easy. 'I've been lucky to have my children. I care about Tereasa and watching her go through her miscarriage and grief was hard. I want her to be a mother. I want her to experience the joy and love I have with my children.'

He just nodded. After a few more formalities, he signed off a form and wished us luck, sending us on our way.

Next, we attended a fertility clinic. I undertook blood tests, an internal scan, and answered questions about past pregnancies and health before we got the green light to proceed. First, we planned a family holiday to unwind and relax before we were to start the next part of the surrogacy process, which would hopefully be pregnancy.

9

Ava's delighted squeals filled the air as she pointed at the passing planes on the tarmac, leaning over Lily to catch a glimpse out the aircraft window. With the engines roaring to life, anticipation buzzed through the cabin as we prepared for take-off. Our destination: Bangkok, aboard flight TG494, before we travelled to Chiang Mai to visit my parents. We were keen to embark on new adventures and create lasting memories together.

Lucas's children were with us; it was their first flight from Australia. I'd worked hard to save for this holiday, and it was the closest thing to a honeymoon we would get. It was an excellent opportunity to spend time together. I was excited to show Lucas's children everything we loved about this spectacular city. Everyone was happy to be together. As we ascended into open skies, I was ready for the time away. Life had been hectic. Faith's surgery had initially been successful, and she returned home to Australia. Thrilled at the news, she had been in good spirits. Then, there had been complications. She was stable and would be okay, but it would take time. Months before, I'd contemplated not going to Thailand.

'Don't be silly,' Faith scoffed. 'Life goes on. You can't put your life on hold for the maybes,' she'd insisted. 'You have to go!'

She was right. As the seatbelt sign switched off and the kids explored the contents of their seat pockets and the airline entertainment system, I felt hopeful everything would be fine. I pulled a book from my luggage and sat back, letting myself unwind, looking forward to an incredible few weeks ahead. We would meet my brother and his family to attend Loi Krathong, the cultural festival of lights. The Thais set off luminescent fireworks that lit the night sky, and little wooden boats shone as they sailed down Chiang Mai's Mae Ping River. The sky glowed with a million lanterns, each a tiny fire. It was the festival of new beginnings, releasing anger, troubles, and negativity as the krathong was lowered into the river and lanterns drifted toward the heavens. It was symbolic as we celebrated new life, marriage, and beginnings.

Hunched over a sink, my eyes were fixed on the bold lines of blood red running towards the drain. I gazed in disbelief, unable to process details as the scene moved, almost in slow motion. Looking up, I saw a sorry figure with dark, broken eyes staring back at me. Startled, I didn't recognise the lowly being standing right before me.

Red, bloodshot eyes, swollen lips, uneven and crusted with brown. A white lace pyjama top, its delicate surface almost entirely shaded in patches of dirty red. Dead and lifeless eyes, filled with self-loathing and resentment, watched me. I recognised those hazel eyes. They were mine, looking back at me from our bathroom mirror, and I hated what I saw.

How had this happened again? What was wrong with me? Was I not better than this? These were questions I'd spent a decade asking.

Lucas returned to our room at 2 am, smelling like booze and unsteady as he walked. He had gone out for a cigarette several hours earlier. Our holiday guesthouse was close to Thapae Road, a popular route for foreigners coming home from the famous night markets. Scammers and sex workers loitered on the corners, calling out to intoxicated tourists wandering home in the early hours.

When Lucas returned, I was both angry and relieved. 'Where have you been?' I challenged him. 'Do you know what time it is?' His eyes were cold, and his response was quick and harsh.

His fist struck my face, knocking me back, hard, into a wall, my legs buckling beneath me. I lay tangled on the floor in the darkness in disbelief. Blood flowed from my nose and lips, defying gravity. In a moment of realisation, I cried, deep sobs overwhelming my body. The shock distorted the sound. I could not breathe; pain shot out from my head and chest in sharp waves. My skin felt hot, the pain radiating up my body.

My youngest daughter, the only child in our room, whimpered at the commotion. I heard Lucas's voice cursing at me from the other side of the room. The lamp clicked, and the room lit up. Silence. He had taken in the reality of the scene before him: the vast pool of blood, my limp body slumped on the cold floor. He gasped audibly, recognising the gravity of what he'd done. I could hear his footsteps approaching carefully. He crouched, his feet by my face. He tugged at my arm frantically.

'Get up. You're fine,' he insisted, in repetition, his voice shaking and laced with panic.

I slowly lifted my head, my cheeks sticky from the blood on the floor.

'Leave me alone. Don't touch me!' I screamed with the last of the defiance I could muster.

I loved this man and hated him for what he had done to us. I'd foolishly believed something was different now that I was his wife, that deep inside, he finally understood the damage he had done.

Last time, he swore it would never happen again.

He didn't move away, and I scrambled against the wall in an involuntary self-protection movement. He grabbed a towel to wipe the thick, red liquid off the floor. There was a knock at the door.

'Mel?' called a voice. 'Is everything okay?'

Shit. It was my brother. How would I explain this? He had seen me arrive on my parents' doorstep several times without explanation, sporting bruises and black eyes, but that had been before the wedding. He'd been there, and, like the rest of the family, he'd bought our well-crafted lie: us being happy. A knock came again, louder, and more urgent, causing the flimsy door to vibrate. I opened it.

I was humiliated but knew Lucas wouldn't touch me if my brother was there. When his eyes adjusted to the dimly lit room, they revealed panic and shock as he took in my distorted appearance – the contrast of crimson on white. I was a broken mess.

Hearing her uncle's voice, Ava began wailing louder from her bed. Every part of me wanted to go to her, to wrap her in my arms and soothe her, but I knew seeing her mother bleeding would frighten her more. Pleading to him, I asked, 'Could you please get Ava?'

He nodded. Tall and solid, he lifted her tiny frame in pink pyjamas into his strong arms and pressed her face to his chest.

Lucas stood silently in the corner against the wall, head down and not daring to meet my brother's bewildered and angry eyes. He walked out into the darkness without a word, his face void of emotion. With a reassuring squeeze of my shoulder after checking I was okay, my brother left to take my daughter, still whimpering, back to his room with his wife and son, leaving me to reflect on what had happened. We had been married for only ten short months.

I'd convinced myself in those mostly uneventful months that things were different. I'd believed being his wife would afford love, kindness, and respect: all the beautiful promises our vows had contained. I was wrong. I had failed.

I married Lucas, believing deep down he was capable of more – that love could heal all wounds – with every fibre of my being. Exhaustion set in, and I showered to remove the drying blood and the stench of failure. I fell asleep just as the morning sun rose behind the blackout curtains. I could not cry, though I longed more than anything to feel the hot, slipping release of tears.

I woke in pain a few short hours later and could hear my husband's deep breathing beside me. Lying still not to rouse him, I lifted my hand to my face. Blood pounded at my temples like the flapping of tiny wings. Tender and limp, my upper lip ballooned over my teeth, and my nose felt like rubber, swollen and numb. When he woke, it was like nothing had happened. He ignored the state of my battered face. The remaining three older children had slept in an adjoining room. I was grateful for the distance, unsure how to cope with their curious eyes and the questions and disapproving looks I would get from my parents if they saw me. Instead, I spent the day in hiding, leaving him to invent a story about me not feeling well.

I knew my brother would reluctantly protect my secret. I spent the day thinking, crying, and sleeping. No matter how much my mind wandered, I returned again and again to a place of uncertainty, confused and tired. At the bathroom mirror, I spread my make-up products across the counter and dabbed at my face with my fingertips, trying to cover the swelling and bruising with foundation and powder.

It looked less and less possible I would be able to cover for him yet again. I texted my family, telling them I wasn't feeling well and needed a rest, and they should go on without me. I told them I was fine, but it wasn't true.

My brother was there in his own quiet way. He looked at me, stealing glances, trying to catch my eye to wordlessly check in on me, to send his support. Some days he lingered nearby, making small gestures – an arm on my shoulder, a gentle smile, bringing me food, a text message checking in – anything to let me know I wasn't entirely alone. Other days, he seemed torn between respecting my wishes and wanting to protect me, hovering at the edges of my world, unsure whether to step closer or stay away. I could see the tension in his jaw, the uncertainty in his eyes, the silent question of how to help without overstepping.

In the midst of my exhaustion, his presence – quiet, careful, watchful – was both a comfort and a reminder of everything I was carrying.

The anger fizzled, and unadulterated grief remained. It was exhausting keeping the weight of secrets, like breaking my back carrying us both uphill. I could not deal with any of it. I didn't have the answers.

The following days were engulfed in a fog of grief as I considered what that night meant for my future, for our marriage. My facial swelling had receded, and my bruising had begun to fade. I tried to be calm for the children. I did not want to ruin their holiday.

Then, I was dealt another bitter blow. I woke up and switched on my phone to receive unexpected news.

'Mel. I'm sorry to message you while you're away. I wanted you to know Faith passed away this morning. I know you were close to her. I'm so sorry. Christina.'

In disbelief, I dropped to the floor of the hotel room, reeling in a depth of pain I'd never experienced before. Heaving sobs wracked my body, and I wailed with bottomless grief. I drowned in a deep, dark ocean and didn't even try to swim. I surrendered to the pain, the sunlight feeling far away and faded. Overwhelming weeping and shallow breathing gave way to slightly deeper restorative breaths. I wasn't ready to say goodbye. There were conversations we still needed to finish.

Did she know I loved her? Did she know how she'd touched people's lives? We had waited for her miracle, anticipating it like a happy ending in an inspiring movie. I believed the recent events were just a twist in her story before she rose over adversity, and we'd return to life as we knew it. It was not to be.

I tried to remember the words of our last conversation. Were they something profound? Something mundane? I searched the room for a sign that would speak to me, a glimmer of hope.

The windows were dull; little light shone through them. There were no voices, music, or sudden revelation – just emptiness. Hope had vanished from my life. It felt bleak and barren. I burned inside, grieving the loss of my confidant as I also grieved my broken marriage. The vows promising things would be different were now shattered into tiny pieces.

The following day, our Thai driver took us to a Buddhist wat suspended atop a lush mountain. Perched over the thick, green forests of Chiang Mai, its gold leaf temples glistened under the blistering midday sun. I embraced the opportunity for wide open spaces and fresh air, any connection to the spiritual world, another world, even one that wasn't mine. I hoped it might bring peace, some anaesthesia so I could say goodbye in my way. I wasn't Buddhist, and no longer knew what I believed, but Faith was spiritual, and I knew she would have loved this place. I cried dozens of times on my way up to the summit. With each wave of grief, I struggled to pull myself together as I clambered off the back of the old red songthaew. I bought a gold-plated bell from a young market vendor and climbed the long stairway to the top. The majestic gold wat stood surrounded by clouds, with coloured glass and mirrored tiles embellishing the statues and ornaments adorning the entrances.

Below were piles of shoes, a mark of respect, as worshipers entered barefoot. As I prepared to go inside, I peeled off my ballet flats. Taking a marker from my bag, I wrote Faith on the tag attached to the bell. Rest in Peace. I hung it from the temple ledge and sat on the stone floor below, feeling a sense of peace. The raging storm within dulled, bringing calm, still waters. I couldn't remember the last time I'd felt this way. Peace had long eluded me, but I knew that to hold onto it, something had to change.

That moment was a catalyst for something, even if I didn't know what it was yet. The days following were filled with solitude, even as I wandered among the busy crowds of the festival, everything devoid of colour and taste. I looked for her face everywhere in the crowded market spaces.

My family and I released glowing lanterns into the open skies, the darkness dotted with fire. The floating lantern candles symbolised letting go of hatred and anger and releasing past transgressions and negative thoughts. I watched the light disappear into the heavens, creating a transcendence. I lay back on the banks of the river, my head resting on a bamboo mat. I gazed up at the glowing lanterns, beacons of hope dotting the skies like stars and waited for something to fall. Everything felt surreal.

We left Thailand a few days later and I packed up my sadness and took it home with us, with the realisation that things within me were changing.

In losing Faith, she'd taught me life was too short to be unhappy. I searched for hope, a way to fix what was dangerously broken. I needed something; I just had no idea what. A silent resolve had grown, and something inside had begun to change.

What hadn't changed, was that I loved him.

As we landed at Brisbane Airport, I was in a haze of grief. My mind was still on Faith, and what I would do without her. She had been my confidant, and I needed her more than ever.

Faith, ever the warrior woman, had refused to accept going out quietly as an option. When she struggled, she smiled and continued as though everything was fine. She had taught me well.

When I fronted up to consider the state of my marriage, I hit a stalemate. Pain ran through my soul like mineral through rock. Any hope this holiday might have been an opportunity to reconnect as a family was gone. This vacation had simply offered the dysfunction a change of scenery.

Losing Faith and watching my marriage crumble simultaneously was devastating. Her funeral was just hours before we landed back in Australia. I deeply regretted not being able to be there to say goodbye, to stand with the people her life had touched. I knew this was the risk we took as mortal humans; when we took love into our lives, our fragile yet fierce hearts could become broken. Her departure had left me in despair, and I was not ready to let her go.

I felt a deep resentment towards the world that carried on like nothing had happened.

All I could do was pledge to exist, to breathe in and breathe out, to get up and go about life until the fog lifted, and I knew what to do next. I kept my eyes on whatever hope I could grasp and focused on continuing the legacy she had left, the one we had started together — Egg Donation Australia. Her legacy was a tree of life that kept giving.

In the weeks before Christmas in 2014, the miracles kept coming. It was a surreal feeling with six babies on the way from my eggs and five recently born. Watching others rise and find joy offered me some happiness and something positive to hold on to.

That Christmas was bittersweet, celebrating miracles and grieving for what was lost. On my mind was the impact of any personal choices I'd made and how they might impact Tereasa. I wanted her to be a mother, and holding my marriage together would keep us moving towards her dream. I would find a way to make it work.

She and I were close; we talked about almost everything, but there were secrets I was not ready to share. Leaving my marriage would undoubtedly leave her dreams in rubble. There was also the shame of failure. We should have been rock solid at ten months of marriage, but we had already begun to fall apart. I did not want Tereasa to see my weakness. I didn't want her to know I wasn't strong enough to walk away from what had been happening.

I did not want to be looked at by her as a victim: helpless, immoral, worthless, weak, or inadequate. God knows I had judged myself harshly enough already. Instead, I'd left breadcrumbs, marking the trail I had walked.

Over the years, I had told different friends little details, small pieces, but never enough for them to put together the entire puzzle. With Tereasa, there was more to lose. If she found out the truth, I knew she would love and put me first, releasing me from my promise.

I didn't want to be released. I was invested, and her dream integrated into mine. I wanted her happiness more than I wanted my own. It was one of the few things I had to look forward to at that point: the lighthouse guiding my ship in the dark and stormy seas. I needed her, and she needed me to be strong, and that was what I would do.

She began an IVF cycle to collect eggs. With her blood clot disorder, it was a risky procedure, but a chance she was willing to take. Her first attempt produced two embryos. Fearing they were not enough, she tried again. Next time, nothing was collected.

Weighing up the risk, she decided not to cycle again herself, instead calling on a donor friend who had offered her eggs. Five little embryos were created. With seven together, we had seven good chances of succeeding, seven little bubbles of hope.

10

My body leaned over the steering wheel, and I wept wildly. I had called a domestic violence women's helpline, desperately needing someone to hear me, to anchor me. The kind operator, a woman, waited patiently. She soothed me as she talked me down from the edge, reminding me to breathe deeply. Her firm but gentle voice was a lifeline when an angry sea swallowed me.

'My name is Sonja. I'm here to listen and to help. I must ask, are you in a safe place right now?'

'Yes,' I answered, still steadying my breathing to respond. 'My husband dragged me across the lounge room by my hair. I had to get out of there. I hate him! I hate him so much.'

She gently asked me my name so she could find my file. 'This is the second time you have called this year. Things have been hard for a while now, haven't they?'

They had, and I knew better. She gave the same advice I'd been given many times before, urging me to save myself, to reach out and get support. To find the strength left inside of me to swim to calmer waters. She was kind and listened. I said troubled words I'd never been brave or desperate enough to say out loud before.

'I've fantasised about killing him. The scene plays on repeat. He comes for me, hatred flashing in his eyes. Instead of just taking it, all weak and pathetic, I finally snap and lash out with a force I didn't know I had – a fury, an unbridled rage building for years. I can almost hear it, the cracking sound of a human skull, as something I hold in my hands strikes his head. I watch him drop. I see his blood. Cold and still. All I feel is an overwhelming sense of relief. Then it's over.' She didn't flinch. There was no gasp of horror, no judgement. Had she heard these wild, desperate words before?

'If something ever happens and I'm arrested, please, can you send these records to my lawyer,' I begged her, distraught and irrational. Is this what my life had become? That I wished my husband was dead? The words I heard from my mouth were those of a broken and desperate woman.

After I had hung up the phone, I sat in silence. What now? Where could I go? The children were still inside and asleep. I had spent so long convincing my family and friends we were going well and marrying Lucas had been the right choice. I didn't want to give them reasons to believe I was wrong. On so many moments like this one, I thought it was the end of us. But it wasn't. He broke my heart and then broke it again while I let him. I didn't know how to let him go.

The relentless navigation of danger had left me mangled. Outwardly I may have looked uninjured, but I was wasting away, my core shattered. If my exterior had matched my soul, I would have limped along, my arms broken and gashed skin hanging loose, scratched and raw. Concealing the truth from others had been exhausting. I slowly cared less about trying to hide my secrets to keep him, to obscure the damage, to yield the polished.

When I returned home, the house was still, heavy with silence, until he saw me and broke down into sobs. 'I'm so sorry,' he said.

'I'll be better. I'll fix this.'

He held me as though I were a grenade, fragile and volatile. I softened for a moment, letting the familiar ache of our shared history surface, but a hardness inside me had taken root – one that would no longer shift. 'It'll be okay. We'll get through this,' I whispered, even as we cried together. Exhaustion finally claimed us, and we fell asleep, bodies pressed close, the night holding both sorrow and an unspoken resolve.

Two days later, I went to see Hannah at the Domestic Violence Centre, still in shock. Something had shifted, and my body felt hollow right down to my bones. The dilemma of what to do had been on my mind, but the indecision circled back, leading me nowhere. I shared with Hannah what had happened with Lucas and how I felt hopeless. When female patients presented at the hospital with various injuries from abusive partners, their stories had stuck with me. They followed me around, their whispers, their echoes getting louder.

I empathised, and inevitably compared myself to their situation, still assuring myself that my circumstances differed. As Hannah spoke gently, she retrieved a page from a folder, holding it out to show me. Its wording ran top to bottom, the font getting more prominent and darker as it ran down the page. There were pencil marks scratched beside the words by other women who had been where I was.

PUSHED

SLAPPED

KICKED

PUNCHED

SEXUALLY ASSAULTED

USE OF WEAPONS
CHOKED
GRIEVOUS BODILY HARM
DEATH

I studied the list to see where I felt I fit before my pencil landed on '**punched**'.

'Wow,' I mused, 'You must get so many women here who go through much worse than I do. I see them come in to work with bloody faces and broken bones, and I feel I'm wasting your time when there are people who need help more than I do. I realise my situation isn't as serious.'

She looked at me with surprise. 'Oh, no, your situation is serious. It's awful. You need to be here.' She picked up the information sheet and showed it to me again.

'You marked punched.' Her pen pointed to the word sitting toward the middle of the list. 'You told me he has punched you in the head many times. You are a nurse? Mel, you know one punch can kill. Does kill.'

She moved her pen down towards **grievous bodily harm**. 'Don't you think this might fit your circumstances better?' she asked, without waiting for an answer.

I swallowed but could not speak as the dread hit my stomach. I could barely look at her. I knew she was right.

Hannah pulled out the 'wheel of abuse' help sheet and put it on the table next to the other. She described the cycle of abuse: the building of tension, the incident occurring, followed by the reconciliation and then the calm. All of this was familiar to me. I knew the pattern by heart.

Hannah explained that as the abuse escalated, we would spend less time in the calm stage before the cycle restarted again. She moved back to the first list. 'So, if this is where you are…' – she pointed to **grievous bodily harm** again with her pen before moving it lower – 'the outcome can't be good. The inevitable end to this cycle is death. Your death.'

She dropped her pen and underlined '**DEATH**' in large, bold font. I stared at the pen markings, taking in what she said and contemplating what they meant. I knew it meant my children would grow up without a mother. It was a thought I couldn't bear. I wasn't sure I truly believed her.

I left her office armed with the fatalistic news – a warning of impending disaster – and it rattled me. Simple, bold language, but what it represented was permanent.

Things had changed. Something had been irreversibly severed. The clock was ticking loudly, the decay, the wastage of precious time. That dangling tooth needed to be ripped out.

I contemplated if it was a risk I could mitigate – something I could do or change that would alter the course of events. I studied Lucas as he watched television, resting a beer on his knee, laughing and absorbed by his show. Thinking about what Hannah had said, I observed him, studying his face, his hands, and his lean body, wondering if he indeed could be capable of doing something as unthinkable as killing me. When he wasn't angry, he was quiet and even gentle.

As he slept, I lay awake, unable to sleep. I watched the outline of his body rise and fall, trying to make sense of the enemy that lay quiet in my midst. Protecting him felt like balancing on a knife edge; on one side, my dreams, and on the other, my deepest despair.

The turquoise waves of Moreton Bay hit the side of the catamaran, splashing upwards on the bow. Our family stood at the front of the vessel, the morning sun streaming towards us as it rose in the east, silhouetting us and casting our shadows onto the deck. The gulls shrieked, and seabirds circled high above the bay.

I rested my arms on the rails, admiring the sandy dunes. Ava wrapped her arms around my waist, burying her head and pigtails into my tummy. Pulling on my shirt, she called for me to pick her up. I did, resting her on my hip and pointing to the boats and the island in the distance. Lucas came up behind us, tugging playfully at her pigtails. 'Daddy, stop!' she squealed, loving every moment of his attention.

Putting his arm around us, we waited as the catamaran slowed to approach the jetty. Stepping down the boardwalk ramp and onto the jetty, we pulled our bags along, and Lucas put Ava on his shoulders, and I held Lily's hand. We checked into the resort, walking to our apartment down amongst the gardens. It overlooked a pool. The weather was glorious, and we spent the days swimming, walking, and quad bike riding, Lily in the passenger seat hanging on tightly to her dad.

He sped down enormous golden dune slopes with Lily on his back, shrieking with laughter as they bounded towards the flats, the sand spraying up as they glided across level ground. At night, we all sat around restaurant tables, the moon illuminating the bay's water as we talked and laughed, giddy with happiness.

We snorkelled the wrecks, swam in the clear water with dolphins and built sandcastles on the beach. Lily tugged at my hand toward the beach to collect buckets of water for her sandcastle moat. That afternoon, Lucas took the girls to the island corner store, returning with a stuffed dolphin and a rainbow Paddle Pop each. Those days I still remember. They were something good. It's essential to hang onto the good wherever you find it.

Months after, in a quiet room of a fertility clinic, a delicate moment unfolded, laden with hope and anticipation as we transferred two tiny embryos, the last remnants of a genetic link for both parents to their child, into my womb.

In the ensuing days, as the hours stretched like taut strings, impatience gnawed at my resolve to wait to do a pregnancy test. I was impatient at the best of times, and here it was, in bold defiance of uncertainty – a strong double line. I shared the news, unable to hold back my excitement. The official blood test the week after confirmed the results. Pregnant.

A flurry of appointments and tests followed, blood tests and a seven-week scan that detected a tiny heartbeat rhythm, was accompanied by a growing sense of excitement as we watched the embryo unfold like a tiny flower. Tereasa watched on excitedly via video call from her home in Hong Kong.

At nine weeks pregnant, I returned for another routine scan, the last before we would graduate to an obstetrician to oversee the remainder of the pregnancy. The door to the examination room opened, and a nurse called out my name. I rose to my feet and followed the nurse down the hallway. Inside, she handed me a gown and blanket. I changed out of my clothes and lay down on the treatment table.

Appearing from behind a curtain, the doctor put on gloves and a mask, checking his notes to confirm our gestation. Nine weeks and two days.

He was quiet while he observed the screen. He told us that he found a gestational sac, but no baby and no heartbeat. Just a small shadow without signs of life.

When you receive news like that, the whole room becomes lifeless. There is no sound, no movement, it's as if no one is breathing and time has stopped. No one wanted to be the first to speak, so he went into a further description of what he saw to defuse the silence.

My mind revisited the weeks before in disbelief, looking for a clue I'd missed, anything suggesting this might be coming. In a movie-like sequence, I replayed the meaningful moments from the first sight of that tiny perfect speck of glowing life twinkling on the same screen, the slight cramp in my abdomen, and the positive pregnancy tests. At seven weeks, there was a little heartbeat flickering on the screen. But now, it was all over.

I caught a look at Tereasa's face. Her eyes were red and puffy. She had been crying.

He reconfirmed the news. 'I'm sorry. The embryo has failed to thrive. Its size is about seven weeks, so it may have been lost after your last scan. You'll need to have a procedure to remove it under a general anaesthetic.' His voice was compassionate.

'Thank you,' I said, trying to be calm, to absorb what I had just heard. A nurse sat beside me, gently explaining the next steps. I was devastated.

I left the clinic and drove home in silence, alone with my thoughts.

I had only one question now. Why? It wasn't fair. Hadn't Tereasa been through enough? Later that night I spoke to Tereasa. I harboured guilt, feeling as though it was my fault. She was sad but radiated strength. Her concern was for me, though it was a big loss for her.

I went to bed early; deep sleep was a respite. I woke the

following morning, the reality of the new day harsh, surging in waves.

I remembered what the nurse had told me: I needed to get a curette to remove the foetus from my uterus. A 'missed miscarriage' she called it. It was such a clinical term for something so personal.

As I was preparing to go in, Dr Ong, who was doing the procedure, looked at me with his temperate eyes. I was in good hands. Waking from the general anaesthetic, I felt empty. Sitting with the disappointment for a few days, I didn't want to dwell on my grief but instead get up and move forward.

Just over a month later, we transferred an embryo from a donor. I was cautiously optimistic. With a proven donor, the odds were better. Again, a home pregnancy test revealed a positive result. Life continued as usual. Two weeks later, while working in the Accident and Emergency department of the hospital, I took a brief bathroom break, finding bright red blood on my underwear. At first, I couldn't understand what I saw. And then the penny dropped, my reaction turned to sorrow. I knew the pregnancy was over; that everything had been lost.

In tears, I told my shift team leader, 'I've already had one miscarriage, and I can't go through this again, but I am! I'm losing the baby, and it's a special baby. . .' I sobbed. She took my hand gently, led me to the triage bay, and directed me to lay on the bed. Moments later, she reappeared with a doctor. There was nothing to be done.

As the blood loss continued heavily, a scan confirmed my worst fears. The pregnancy was over. Lying on the hospital bed, I stared at the white speckled ceiling. This room had seen a lot. My uterus cramped with intensity, my lower back ached as I felt my body shedding itself from the inside as gravity took over. I felt what was left of the baby leaving my body, with only monitors beeping and my tears for company.

I went home to be alone, curling up in the shower as I continued to miscarry, my sobs echoing through the bathroom. Crimson discoloured the water as it flowed towards the drain in linear stripes. On that cold floor, the exhaustion and grief finally hit home: Tereasa's grief, my grief, the loss of these babies, my health, time, and the loss of our dreams.

I couldn't convey my pain to Tereasa. I shielded her from it. She had her own to carry. I could not talk to my husband either; it was not his child. He might have grown resentful and changed his mind with pressure or stress, withdrawing his support. The surrogacy had been on the condition it did not overly impact his life.

Sarah was a lifeline. She called faithfully to check how I was, even when I withdrew into myself. Her voice at the end of the line was comforting. She could read me, knowing exactly what to say and when to listen. She offered distraction, making me cry with laughter to forget my pain when things weren't going well.

Miscarrying a baby that was not mine presented a unique situation, one difficult to identify with. Can one genuinely grieve a loss that isn't theirs? The trails of complex thought offered an endless maze of emotions.

We had no answers but many questions. Was it my fault? Was my uterus faulty? Could it be the sperm? The eggs? Were we just unlucky? There was no way to know. This second pregnancy was shorter, but the loss was far more challenging. It brought daily reminders as the bleeding went for weeks. It took a toll on all of us. Some friends were adamantly against us trying again, asking when enough was enough as they were concerned about my deteriorating health. I insisted I could look after myself and I would decide when I'd had enough of trying. I wasn't there yet. I still wanted to keep trying. Tereasa offered me an out many times, but I refused. If she was strong enough to continue, so would I.

We had two remaining embryos. We tried again, transferring both, praying for a break. It was our last chance. For a third time, I was pregnant again, but I struggled to feel the enthusiasm or get attached to something that felt elusive. We tentatively acknowledged milestones as they came but took a wait-and-see approach.

At eight weeks, it happened again. At a routine scan, it was all over. It wasn't to be.

Again, we had to let go. I was scheduled for another curette. I sat in a hospital room in a blue cotton gown as Sarah looked on, concerned. How calm I felt surprised me. I could handle this. This would not bury me.

We took selfies on our phones from the waiting room as I went to go in, trying to find some humour in an otherwise shitty situation. If we didn't laugh, we would cry.

After the procedure, and I went back to square one, I took a break. The losses had taken their toll. I was emotionally tired; my body had paid the price. My weight had increased from both fertility drugs and comfort eating. I felt unhealthy and worn out.

It was a mindfuck. Every. Single. Day. I had been scanning the skies for approaching storms, hypervigilant. I insisted I was fine. For more than a year, I'd insisted I was fine, but I was not fine. We decided to take a few months' break. After regaining our strength, we would try again. We were down but not out.

Weightless in a pool of blue water, I floated on my back, eyes closed. The gentle murmur of my daughters' voices carried over the water as they splashed and played nearby. I could hear chatter in an Asian dialect, the calls of unfamiliar birds, and the rustle of palm trees blowing in the breeze. Opening my eyes, I took in the scenery. The giant grey cityscape towered over our inner-city tropical oasis, neon signage iridescent, lighting up the dusk skyline.

Hong Kong city was both strong and beautiful. During the daytime, we wandered the alleyways, discovering tiny eateries, local markets, and sprawling green spaces, our affection growing for this amiable city. It was a curious affair to observe Tereasa in her surroundings. She was a foreigner but navigated the buzzing metropolis with confidence. She was a chameleon anywhere she went; her home was wherever she made it. I respected her courage and resilience.

She had shown that quality in spades in the months before, the highs and lows making for a stomach-turning ride, but I knew she, like me, was committed to finishing this. Taking a break from the physical toll the last few months had taken on us was an opportunity to rest and contemplate.

Like the Chinese lanterns hanging across the street in front of her building, we were suspended in time. I had lost three pregnancies, and others Tereasa herself had endured. It was now a process of elimination to work out why. As much as we tried not to give thought to trying again, we couldn't help ourselves. We often found our way back to talking strategy on the afternoons spent lazing around the pool as the children played. What had we missed? What could we do differently?

2013 had been a challenging year. The dream felt as far away as ever. The days were off-limits to anything other than adventure.

We caught a tram to the city's peak, the tall mountain walkways and rainforest greenery over the dense city. We took the girls to Disneyland, posing for photographs with their favourite characters and going on rides until the park showed signs of closing. The children had been good sports. They knew what we were trying to achieve and wanted it for Tereasa too. We broke the information into kid-sized pieces and sheltered them from the harsher details, but they knew this was a dream project under construction. We all wanted to make their honorary Aunty Tereasa a mother.

It was an opportunity to reconnect with Tereasa and my children and my parents. They flew across from Thailand to meet us in Hong Kong and finally meet Tereasa.

My mother, who had not entirely understood why I would want to be pregnant with someone else's baby, grew fond of Tereasa as the days passed and appeared to finally understand. Her expression of sentiment was simple yet poignant. As we prepared to cross a road, and Tereasa held the girls' hands ahead, Mum said to me, 'If I had a uterus, I'd give it to her too.' She was referring to both her hysterectomy and fondness for Tereasa. It felt nice to have her support.

During our stay in Hong Kong, we rented a small apartment nestled in a bustling local marketplace. Red lantern lights cast a warm glow over the narrow streets, while the air was filled with the rich, savory aromas of local dishes sizzling on the woks and grills of street vendors. The vibrant energy of the market, with its colourful stalls and the sporadic clatter of cooking, created a lively backdrop to our days, blending the sounds and scents. At night, I would sit with my mother, and we would talk about what she was doing in Thailand and her new job teaching children. The dynamic of our relationship had shifted, two women with two parallel lives, more of an adult and less of a child. Those weeks away were good for my soul and to rebuild my strength. I found it strange that I did not miss Lucas like I had when previously apart. I thought of him but did not feel lonely.

As we walked the paths of the green trails ascending the city skyline and overlooking the skyscrapers below, I wished he had been with us to witness the beauty of it. At the same time, the absence of walking on eggshells was liberating, peaceful, and I felt no rush to return home.

After much contemplation, I offered to both carry the pregnancy and donate my eggs to Tereasa, which is called traditional surrogacy. The thought process had been relatively straightforward but had taken time to consider the emotional complexities. I had been willing to give her my eggs; I'd been willing to carry her child. This way, I would give her both.

Some might feel it is heartless, as though a surrogate would either feel nothing or too much for the child she is 'giving up'. Others questioned the bond with the child during pregnancy and whether they could go through with it. It was the question people asked again and again, looking at me with pity. Would my body keep the score knowing that the child was of my flesh?

Initially, I did too. How would I feel? Could I give up a child when it was born? Was it possible to compartmentalise the emotions of ethics of such an act?

It was something I pondered before the last of the donor embryos failed. Traditional surrogacy was an insurance policy; one I hoped we wouldn't have to use. As time went on, the uncertainty faded, and the choice came with a greater sense of clarity.

I'd already donated eggs and met children born from my eggs. There was genetic connection, yet I felt nothing emotionally, apart from a fondness I would feel for any of my friends' children. I was sure I would be fine. We were back standing at the beginning after three heartbreaking miscarriages with no answer. It was our best chance of success.

The journey had come with high costs - emotionally, physically, mentally, and financially for Tereasa. It felt like the right choice. Traditional surrogacy presented a new way forward; one I hoped would afford us some breathing room. The girls and I returned home to Australia and to our lives. We would try again early the following year. The new year offered a beacon of hope.

11

'He did what?' I stammered, disbelief and anger twisting in my chest. The pit of my stomach flipped with a familiar sense of anxiety as I took in the news.

'Yeah, she's at the police station now. She's really upset,' Sarah said, her voice heavy with concern. 'I'm going to see her this afternoon. Maybe you could come too?'

'Of course,' I replied, unsure what else to say. 'I'll meet you there.'

A dear friend – one who I had walked life's milestones with, been there for the birth of her children, stood beside through ups and downs – needed me. I set out on the hour-long drive, my mind laden with heavy thoughts.

Weeks earlier, I had driven the same journey. I sat beside her as she cried, tearfully explaining what had happened, twisting her engagement ring around her delicate finger in distress. I listened, hearing my own story in hers. She was looking for answers, confused and lost. Torn, I didn't feel qualified to offer advice. Everyone else would say to her what my instinct screamed. Run! Run away while you can. Don't you know you're so much better than this?

But my heart battled against that advice. I would be a hypocrite for speaking my mind. I understood her pain and her confusion at not understanding how a man who loved her could lay his hands on her, how a man who said she was his everything could utter cruel and unkind words. I knew it all too well. The weight the questions could carry. With nowhere for my feelings to escape to, I imploded. Silent and serene on the outside, inside I was detonating. Gathering my courage, I let go of my secret life, fiercely guarded to protect the man I loved. She needed to hear it.

'See this scar?' I asked, pointing at my face, my fingertips tracing a length of raised skin from my lips to my cheek. My tongue instinctively traced the other side, feeling the scarring there too. She nodded silently, her expression curious.

'Lucas did this. I had to get stitches at the hospital. He drove me there. I was bleeding everywhere.'

She looked horrified, her head down, but eyes fixed firmly on me.

'And you remember how I told you something had happened in Thailand, and I said I wasn't sure if it would change everything but couldn't tell you what?' She nodded. 'We fought. He broke my nose.' I continued before she could speak.

'I have taken the kids and stayed in caravan parks in the middle of the night. It has been like this for years, and it's been hell at times. I have had black eyes and bruises. I have hung in there for dear life. I have held on to our family and my marriage with everything I have. It has been hard. I want to see in him the man I know he is deep down when times are good… when we are happy. I've hung on for those moments. And for now, things have been good for a few months. But it breaks you. It devastates your soul. You have got to know staying with him will be tiring. It's an ongoing battle neither of you will win. It won't be easy. If he wants to change, he will, but he will have to want to and work at it every day. I can't tell you what to do. The next part is your decision.'

Looking up, I saw both their eyes locked on me with shaken expressions. 'How long has this been going on for, Mel?' Sarah asked, her eyes welling with tears.

'Over ten years now. It has only now started to get better. I'm hopeful things are different. If it ever happens again, I will leave.' I heard my own words; they marked a line in the sand. I wondered if they sounded resolute. I'd set a benchmark. A red line I could not cross.

They knew everything now. The minute he hit me again, I would have to leave. But the truth was, I wasn't sure I would.

'You shouldn't put up with living like this, my friend. You are strong. You are better than this. You're stronger than me. It breaks you down gradually. It rips your self-worth apart. I want better for you. I know I have no right to say that, and it makes me a hypocrite. But you are my friend, and I love you.' The tears welled in my eyes as I heard my own words.

I hoped she heard what I'd said, and I hadn't exposed my dark secrets for nothing. But if I had to sacrifice my shame for her wellbeing, it was worth the risk. Whatever she decided, I wanted the best for her. Though humiliating, I felt another emotion. Unexpectedly, it was liberation. A weight had lifted.

Yet, as I drove home, old memories circled my head like a vulture. I knew this would be something more significant. Like the time before I had gone to her, she was angry and sad, contemplating her future. She made plans to go. She made plans to move on with her life. She blasted his actions on social media to her friends and family. Then, she did what so many women who experience violence at the hands of their partners do. She went back to him.

Her choice was not the catalyst for a massive change for her, but it was for me. Her many friends and family were horrified at her decision. I was, too. She was beautiful and intelligent. She was strong, far stronger than I was. Why was she putting up with this? I had no right to be upset – people in glass houses.

I had confided in another friend the year before, after a fight with Lucas had yet again crossed the line. I picked up the phone to talk to her. I told her what had happened: the abuse, the injuries, our chequered history.

It took courage to speak up and tell her. She replied with a question I will never forget: 'That's terrible. What did you do to upset him?'

I was speechless.

'I mean, he seems so nice. Are you sure?' I could hear shock and disbelief. She worked to reconcile what I had told her: a man who could be so charming and generous in outside company could be a monster behind closed doors. A man who would beat his wife. Frighten her, control her. Society fails to grasp that both truths can coexist.

Her response gave me insight into the views of others. People might not believe me. No wonder so many choose to remain silent. With some reflection, I realised I was guilty of the same. I'd felt frustration towards my friend for staying, rather than towards her husband for not keeping his hands to himself.

I was black with anger at myself. Denial was a far easier path to travel. My reaction consumed me. Sad and angry, the emotion resounded in the deepest parts of me. I was porous, and they infiltrated every layer of my being. It was a wild horse, a free-roaming brumby. If I didn't rein it in and ride, harnessing the anger into something constructive, it would drag me along. This was her battle to fight, with fear, anger, uncertainty – even love. And yet it was mine, also.

I struggled under the weight of indecision. Carrying secrets affects your breathing, your clarity, your speech. Their dead weight, their, ties you up in invisible knots. Does one keep secrets or do your secrets keep you?

The feeling became obsessive as I sought distraction, desperately needing to do something as anger and anxiety burned in me. I turned to the internet for information, a search returning an organisation: RizeUp, that created sanctuary homes for women fleeing domestic violence.

Seeing the beautiful homes they made, I signed up. It gave the emotion somewhere to go, to channel the energy into something good. This decision was cathartic.

In March, I unloaded a furniture trailer at a small apartment, a haven home. Everything going into it was donated by the goodwill of strangers – from the furniture in the rooms to the food in the refrigerator.

As I moved a box inside, my teammate Belinda held the door open. She was a pretty blonde, a mum with a son. Her ponytail bounced as she moved, energetic and friendly. I was pleased to be paired with her for the project. Our stories had similarities, more than we both understood at the time. As the house came together, detail by detail, I felt a growing sense of pride. The home was for a mother and her two small boys.

We decorated the boys' rooms in little blue car designs, with rugs, toys, and books. I hoped the mother's life was destined to be brighter and better. This kindness by strangers meant she knew people stood behind her, having her back, and it would inspire her not to give up. After seven long days of work, it was complete. Every detail was beautiful, from the fresh-cut flowers in a vase to throw pillows on beds and pictures in delicate frames.

The bedrooms, bathroom, and kitchen held everything a young family could need. Before handing over the keys to the social worker, we sat, reflecting on the conversations and contemplation we had as we worked. We, two young mums, had something more in common than the obvious, wondering if those we were helping were like us – women from abusive relationships. We could not pity the unknown woman because the difference between her and us was she had been courageous enough to walk away. Who knew how many times she had tried before? If only I had courage as she did.

Belinda opened up about her own marriage, sharing a story similar to mine. Maybe our isolation meant we could no longer see our reflection in other people's eyes, indicating what was and wasn't normal. In each other and that week of work, something switched. How easily we had concealed painful truths, and veiled vast mountains.

We understood then what we hadn't before, but still didn't know what to do about it. I spent time slowly chipping away at the truth, layer by layer, terrified to cause a collapse. My marriage had been stationary for a few months. There was no feeling of deep love and connection, nor immediate danger or devastation. Ingrained in habit, we were used to discomfort parading as structure, as routine, on time like an express train, down the same predictable lines. Sudden upheaval would expend emotional energy that I didn't have in me. Assuming we had time to figure it out, we returned to our lives.

As winter came, we decided to move to a new home. Lucas and I had talked about it for months, though I knew it was me who needed it most. I felt restless, caught in a cycle that had grown too familiar, weighed down by old routines and the ghosts of what had been. Our home, once a sanctuary, had begun to feel like a mirror of all the parts of my life I was ready to leave behind. I craved a fresh canvas, a space that belonged less to the past and more to the person I was trying to become. The decision came quietly, but with a fierce certainty – I would move us to a new neighbourhood, not merely for a change of scenery, but to reclaim a sense of possibility, a sense of myself.

Pulling the door closed on our empty house, I said my goodbyes. The move was complete, the truck gone. There was no regret in this farewell as I prepared to hand back the keys. Taking one last glance at the house I called home for seven years, I felt overwhelmed.

Nostalgia permeated every corner of the house – so many ghosts and secrets. The walls were an old book, absorbing a little of the humanity of all that touched its pages. There were happy memories but also those of anguish and despair. My identity felt entwined in the place, and all it represented. I hoped to shed it like old skin.

Closing my eyes, I was flooded with memories of packing for camping trips and the trampoline springs squeaking in the backyard as the kids played. I remembered standing on the lawn looking at our house with such hope before we moved in seven years before, trusting it would bring better days for us. I left a little of myself behind as I drove away for the last time. We moved to a nearby suburb; our plans for a new start beginning with the best intentions. This time it was less about we and more about me. I wanted more from life and had begun to make changes slowly.

That autumn, our neighbourhood was beautiful, its leafy gardens and sprawling green spaces leading to playgrounds and a recreation centre – a resort-sized pool with bike paths that wrapped around the lakes, filled with ducks and their young. It represented the life I wanted for myself. Removing family photos from cardboard boxes, I wiped off a thin layer of dust from the frames and set them on the bookshelf.

The first few weeks in the new house were a blur of unpacking, arranging, and finding our rhythm. The rooms felt unfamiliar but full of possibility. Life felt quieter somehow, yet beneath the surface, a tension lingered – small, subtle, almost imperceptible – like a tremor before an earthquake. I tried to hold onto the sense of new beginnings, but the past has a way of seeping in, uninvited and relentless.

Then it happened.

'Stop it, leave Mum alone!' cried Lily, her words teeming with fear and desperation, her eyes wet with tears. Although small, she was fierce. Her voice created enough surprise that he loosened his grip and stood back, glowering at her and then at me, contemplating what to do next.

This was not the life I wanted for any of us. My gaze moved between him and my daughters. Lily was on her feet, eyes wide and body tense. Her courage had won even though her voice shook. I had cradled her as a newborn, alone in her nursery with the lights of her mobile and the soft, lacy threads of her linen, promising I'd keep her safe. I had failed.

A decade later, we found ourselves trapped in the same bad dream. Her determination to protect me was unwavering. I felt a mix of pride and horror; after all, she was just a child, and this burden wasn't hers to carry. Her eyes locked onto mine, searching, fully aware of what was unfolding. In that moment, she reminded me of a younger version of myself, witnessing the same brokenness and dysfunction in the adults around her. There needed to be a circuit breaker; we had to leave. The police were on their way.

For me, this was both a safety net and something that riddled me with angst. I moved in front of Lily, watching him intently, trying to predict his next move. Scooping up his car keys, he headed for the front entrance, slamming the screen door behind him. The distinctive sound of his diesel four-wheel drive roared to life and faded as he drove off into the night.

I called the police to inform them he had left. They told me they would send a car regardless.

In the lounge room with the girls, I held my emotions together, pulling both towards me and trying to soothe them. Everything would be okay, I told them, stroking their heads. But would it be? I was lying to all of us. Nothing was okay. We were all in serious trouble.

Having moved into this house just weeks before, it had already started to collect the same gloomy memories we left behind at the last house, forming like spiders weaving webs in corners. At this rate, this house would never be home either.

I tucked the girls into bed and stroked their heads goodnight; they gazed at me, looking for reassurance. 'We will go to the park and play tomorrow. I love you,' I promised, offering a soothing smile. They nodded and rolled over to sleep.

I went outside to get some fresh air, feeling the walls were closing around me. Pulling the door shut behind me, I sat, the breeze brushing my face, cool and consoling.

A dam of tears burst, the exhaustion and sadness giving way. I took out my phone, staring at its glowing screen, trying to make out words through my tears. There were already texts and missed calls from Lucas. I ignored them, not ready to talk. Instead, I messaged Sarah. She knew me and would talk me down from the edge if anyone could.

'It's over.' SEND.

That was it. It was out now.

My phone lit up with a message. 'Are you okay?' came the reply.

'No. The old Lucas is back.' I typed. 'Angry Lucas. I can't do this anymore.'

The phone rang, her name flashing on caller ID. As I answered, I struggled to breathe and find words that made sense. They poured out, the events painting a picture of my broken world.

'What are you going to do, Mel?' she asked slowly, her voice gentle.

'I don't know,' I replied flatly, tired.

'I've tried so fucking hard to fix this. So hard. We have done counselling so many times, and he's done anger management classes. Nothing has worked. It doesn't get any better. It's not going to change, is it?' I asked, already knowing the answer.

Sarah was silent. Her steady breath whispered through the phone at the end of the line. She didn't need to say anything.

'I'm here for you, always,' she offered, emotional. 'If you want to come and stay, there's room for you anytime.'

'Thank you.' I felt exhausted.

After I hung up, her words were suspended in air, hovering amid the fireflies. The number of missed calls multiplied, along with text messages. Lucas wanted to know if the police had come yet.

'I'm tired,' I told him. 'The police aren't here, and I'm going to bed.'

Minutes later, as I prepared to climb into bed, the front door clicked. He'd returned. Pausing at the door as he entered the room, downcast, he gazed at the floor, his steely blue eyes bloodshot like mine.

'I'm sorry,' he offered. His voice was emotional.

'You're sorry?' I repeated in disbelief, my eyes welling with tears. 'Like every other time you have said those same words, nothing has changed. I don't believe you. You have ripped our family apart. I'm tired and broken, and I can't do this anymore. I can't. I fucking won't!'

I was exasperated. 'These kids deserve better! I deserve better.'

'I know,' he responded, tearing up but offering nothing more.

Switching the light off, we lay in silence. He reached for me, stroking my arm. I felt numb. Then came a knock on the door – the police.

Switching on a lamp, Lucas stared over at me in panic. 'Please send them away. I'll go hide in the spare room,' he pleaded, his eyes filled with fear. He moved quickly, disappearing.

I opened the front door. The police stood on the step, examining me with concern. I stepped out, pulling it shut behind me. 'My kids are sleeping. He's not here,' I offered.

The female officer eyed me up and down, disbelief evident on her face.

'What happened tonight?' she asked.

I was dismissive. 'It was an argument. It's fine now,' I promised, trying to sound convincing. I couldn't meet her eye.

I was frightened of him but frightened for him too.

Covering for him was how it always went. I was ashamed and angry at him, and at myself. Why did I protect him? On our wedding day, he had promised to love and protect me always. Instead, I needed protection from him.

The officer eyed me firmly. 'Melissa? We've read through your history. There's some serious stuff. Have you got help?' she asked.

'Yeah, I've been seeing the Domestic Violence Centre since 2008.'

She looked at me, stunned. '2008? And you're still here?'

She paused before staring squarely at me with a no-nonsense expression. 'You need to do something. You are going to lose those kids. Do you hear me? The Department of Child Safety will take them. This can't keep happening. I'm going to send through another referral. You have yourself and your kids to consider. Do you understand what I'm saying? You need to do something about this.'

'I know.' My eyes met hers, conceding my position. There must have been a sign of strength confirming I heard what she'd said. She handed me a card, requesting I call again if there were any further incidents. I nodded before closing the door. I was left standing in the darkness. The officers' footsteps receded, followed by the thud of car doors closing and the crackle of chatter on the police radio.

I found Lucas hiding in a cupboard, his eyes anxious as he saw me.

'Are they gone?'

I could only nod before turning around and moving back to our room. I climbed into bed for a second time, and reality landed. It was lightning and I was earth. I cried, sobbing, barely able to breathe. I could feel bruising on my body. It ached. Lucas held me, wanting to connect with me, but I recoiled at his touch. There was no easy out; there was no pretending. I needed to work this out and was running out of time. I eventually drifted off to sleep, the exhaustion kicking in.

Something had finally snapped, a piece of me hanging by a thread for so long. It had been not even two weeks since hearing the officer's warning; I couldn't erase her words from my mind. I was sitting alone in the car after dropping the girls at school. I couldn't feel anything. My head was tired. It was like everything was behind a thick pane of glass. There was little space for rumination of self. I'd retreated into motherhood, but trying to maintain the facade in front of the children was so consuming. The constancy of their needs, their relentless need for attention, connection, and security kept me firmly present. But this plan was not foolproof. As hard as I tried to keep up the outward show, the children knew something was amiss, asking questions I hadn't figured out the answers to yet. Something had switched. I looked at Lucas and felt nothing. I had no respect, and any love had tapered off to a slow trickle. Unlike during the rest of our relationship, I no longer felt sorry for him. When you see things differently, it's hard to unsee them again.

Lily had a pet bird, a cockatiel, that escaped when Lucas asked her to clean his cage outside, rather than indoors as she usually had. He slipped through a gap, flying up into the surrounding trees. She was devastated seeing and hearing her bird perched up in the branches, unable to retrieve him. She cried, her expression one of blind panic, perhaps afraid that she would be in trouble for the accidental release. Overwhelmed, she cried out to her dad in frustration, asking why he'd made her take the cage outside.

His reaction, his fury had been terrifying, like a shooting star, burning wildly, crazy and out of control. He stood inches from her face, screaming, his words mangling her self-esteem. I intervened, shielding her behind me as I raged at him. It was like my body had a trigger. I sat there ablaze, pushed so far that there was nothing to lose. I felt dangerous, a bomb timer counting down, ready to go off. The fact this was terrifyingly unhealthy had not escaped me.

I went to see Hannah. I needed support and resources to help me move forward with leaving. I considered taking the girls and moving to a women's refuge in a new town far away. They would have to move schools, I'd have to leave my job, my friends and support network. I was overwhelmed by the feeling of injustice that we would lose everything, because he had taken an axe to our life, destroying our family while he destroyed himself. I planned to leave quietly, trying to be sensible, organising my finances and looking for housing options. I recognised the seriousness of my situation and knew it was time to go. I packed up the kids and left to stay with Sarah.

Lucas and I argued by text message. I had run out of reasons to try and threw jagged words at him. 'Your temper! You NEVER get help even though things keep happening. Lily and the bird. How has this become our normal? You're going to kill me one day. I can't be afraid. I can't take it. It's not how things are supposed to be. You don't get it, hey? It's happened our entire relationship.'

He offered no reaction, retreating. I realised that after over a decade, this was our routine. I arrived at Sarah's doorstep as midnight approached. She welcomed us, gathering pillows and blankets and finding us a bed. I held myself together on the drive, not wanting the girls to see me cry. The messages on my phone were angry and threatening before switching to loving and begging for us to come home. I was tired in every single way a human being could be.

We sat on her back patio; the children tucked safely into bed. Sarah looked at me with her yellow-hazel cat eyes, rubbing my shoulder. I cried, tears coming from a boundless well within me. I told her everything. She was as incredulous and pissed off and loving as I needed her to be.

When I calmed, I found my voice. 'It's over. I can't go home. Everything is fucked. My marriage is over.' Any window of hope had closed. I no longer knew the man I married. The good moments we shared were white, the bad ones black, all crushed and blended until everything became a mottled, gloomy charcoal grey. The bad far outweighed anything good. The man I'd known had slowly disappeared. The weight of his anger and the heaviness of his hurt left him misshapen and unfamiliar, until we were left with a stranger who was both callous and unkind. For years, I had looked to any reason to stay, with infinite hope things could be better. Now, I searched for something to hold on to and came up empty.

There were so many empty conversations filled with empty words. Now, there was just one remaining. Goodbye.

12

The picturesque Sydney sunshine glistened across the city harbour, the day, off to a perfect start. The waterways were alive with huge passenger ferries and tourist cruise boats passing as masses of seagulls darted overhead, searching for morsels of food left behind by the hordes of tourists. The lively sounds of buskers playing and children squealing with excitement filled the air, creating an infectious energy. Darling Harbour buzzed with activity, its restaurants and wine bars teeming with locals and tourists. Along the waterfront, sprawling parklands stretched out, dotted with cafés where students and corporate professionals, engrossed in their work, sipped espressos with headphones in, their focus unwavering as they typed away on laptops. Nearby, young families relaxed on blankets, enjoying picnics while their children played in the park.

It was the perfect setting for a day I looked forward to. I walked across the grass finding a group of familiar faces, their eyes lighting up as they welcomed me. Under a poinciana tree, red flowers fell with the breeze. I sat on the picnic rug beside them, and they embraced me.

We talked and laughed for hours, reminiscing. Eight children were there, born from my donations, with another on the way, a bump under their mother's sundress. These women were some of my favourite people in the world. Despite living in several different states, we were all together in one place. It was a welcome distraction from my life, a place where I could feel sunshine in every sense of the word. I was overwhelmed by the pride of what brought us here together. I revelled in the moment as I captured mental memories, promising myself it would be a day I would never forget.

I looked at the children playing under their parents' watchful eyes. Each child was once an impossible dream to the parents who longed for them. I remembered the first time I had met them, some in hidden-away coffee shops or on the phone, their voices etched with nerves. Fear and hopelessness were a common theme, many of them telling me this mountain had seemed too high to climb and the possibility they might one day join a mother's group or do a school run seemingly impossible. And yet, here we were.

We looked like any other group of families on a weekend picnic. No one would guess the miracle story behind every family sitting there. I watched these women hold their children's hands as they walked. What bonded me to them was my friendship with their mothers.

My hopes were high as I watched Tereasa play with the children who had taken to her as my children had. She would make a beautiful mother. We were close to starting our next attempt at surrogacy. I hoped this would finally be the one we were waiting for, and we could make some magic for her, too.

These remarkable women's stories and lives had just begun, holding endless possibilities. From them, I learned that sometimes things fall apart before they fall together. I had faith that with persistence and hope, my life would also make peace with itself. It would just take some time.

I agreed to attend marriage counselling at Lucas's request. It had been the thing that had clenched the condition of his moving out. The domestic violence service informed me they could assist having him removed from the property through the courts, but that road was my last resort. Desperate for peace, I acceded to this request.

We had gone to a marriage counsellor; one he had chosen out of a newspaper. It was then I had met Tony, the calm, gentle man who led me through the howling winds, whipped up dust blinding my steps, directing me toward shelter. He was a voice of reason. I saw his compassion and it restored something that had been broken, reminding me that good men could be a safe harbour. That all I had known was not all there was to see. I had been swimming in muddied waters, but he had thrown me a lifeline of integrity – of hope – and I had reached for it. I was finally strong enough to walk away. There had been times I wanted to run, leaving only to return weakened, enticed by promises, reminded of better days. This time had to be different. It had been coming for a long time, and now it was done.

I feel there is more to explain: a subclause of note. This isn't a story of a good wife and a bad husband. I wasn't always easy to live with. I can be stubborn, emotional, and avoidant. I can give the silent treatment, but that quiet pain was loud. In a narrative story, there is the protagonist and an antagonist – the hero and a villain, the good guys, and bad guys. In life there are hurt people who hurt people. The walking wounded who are broken, and those who strike out to protect themselves, seeing enemies everywhere. I was a paper doll with a million tiny cuts, wondering how I would ever feel whole again. I wasn't my best self in that marriage. I wasn't always kind. I harboured resentment, anguish, contempt, bitterness, defensiveness… and towards the end, rage.

Maybe this is a story of two contrary humans, young and badly broken, trying to bridge a cavernous gap but unable to survive each other's changes. Many things, once broken, are hard to mend, and the least visible scars last the longest. To save my marriage and our family, I abandoned myself. I set myself on fire to keep him warm. If it wasn't for my children, I would have sacrificed myself for longer. I'd been trying to save the marriage, but I needed to save myself.

I flashed back to the devastating fight in the Thai hotel room. Since that night, I had seen a change in me. It signalled the beginning of the end, and I could not ignore the signs of impending disaster. I began hiding kitchen knives far back in their drawer, out of sight, trying to anticipate what would happen next, spinning into pre-emptive damage control. I hid money and essential documents, assembling a 'go bag' in case of an emergency, a contingency plan for escape should the worst eventuate. I noticed my swift retreat when his demeanour changed, like seeking shelter after a sudden wind change, signalling the approach of a perfect storm.

But things were different now. It was time to take back my life. I removed my wedding ring, holding it momentarily before tucking it into my pocket. Letting go can be the hardest thing you'll ever have to do.

It was 10 pm. The house was quiet, and I sat curled up on the sofa in sweatpants and socks. Ava had fallen asleep in my arms, her exhausted head sunk into my side. Her long, dark eyelashes, her fair skin, and pink lips relaxed as she slept peacefully. With the volume low, the credits rolled down the television screen, barely illuminating the dim room. Switching it off and tossing the remote aside, my eyes adjusted to the darkness. Tracing her soft skin with my fingertips, I knew I'd taken the first step to make right so many wrongs.

I want a divorce were words not spoken recklessly, nor did they come without regret. I battled with breaking our family apart, but as I looked at my daughter's pretty face, I knew she deserved better. If she grew up thinking what she had known was normal, I'd never forgive myself. It was during these quiet moments alone when I grieved the loss of the dream of a family, one with two loving parents and their children. Together. Happy.

It would have been easier for love to fade, dying a slow death, finally abandoned, and accepted as gone. I did not let go easily and this quality sometimes felt like a curse. Despite what Lucas had done, I missed him.

How did I put into words that when I left my abuser, I had lost my friend, my confidant? How could I explain that the abuser was only part of who he was? How could I explain that to myself?

Grief was a dark smudge underneath my eyes, contrasting my pale skin. I had not been sleeping well; getting on with life was a struggle. He was a ghost, gone now, and I wasn't permitted to mourn him.

Explaining it to someone outside of the relationship was complex and impossible. No one could understand how love, hate, fear, and comfort could simultaneously coexist. He had peeled layers away, leaving me a shell of my former self. I wasn't even sure I loved myself anymore. When had that stopped? It had happened so gradually I'd failed to catch it.

The biggest tragedy had not been the loss of our marriage but that I'd lost myself.

I had things to keep me focused, including the job of helping Tereasa. I called her and had the most honest conversation I had ever had. I shared the intricate and painful details of my life transparently. She listened, considering every word. I gave her a chance to opt out, to change her mind. She wanted to know if I was okay. Was I really okay?

Her questions were raw and candid, asking about me, my heart, and my safety. I was honest and told her everything, laying my soul bare. Perhaps she heard the strength, the resolve, the fight. She knew me – the real me.

We chose then and there to keep moving ahead. I thought if I woke up each day, breathed in and out, cared for the kids, cared for myself, and then went to bed again, that one day I would wake up, and it would all hurt less and less until it did not.

'Get through each day one at a time. Take one step, and then take another. Then one day you will look back and recognise how far you've come,' she told me. 'You are strong enough to get through this. It will just take some time to heal.'

How long? When? I wanted to know.

For me, grief had occasioned a type of disappearance. I withdrew from people, muted, and muffled, toning myself down to a quieter composition. For someone who had once lived in colour, with so much to give and so much to say, I had become more restrained and subdued. I needed that cocoon of withdrawal to understand what had happened to me and to be able to process the event and sift through the broken pieces to see if I could salvage anything worth keeping. Was there a turning point, a magic number of days, when I would wake up and this grief would not break me any longer? How I wanted that.

I dreamed of the day things would finally be different. The day I loved and was loved in return, a life without fear, pain, and isolation. I dreamed of one day waking up beside a man who loved me, feeling happy and at peace. It seemed an impossible dream. Did this kind of love exist?

Maybe it was a fantasy, but I clung to it, unwilling to let go. I had something to hope for, to believe in. No one would take it away. I wrote about these thoughts in my journals to give the emotions I was feeling a voice. Through this, I could siphon off resentment and anger, alleviate the fear, soothe the sadness, and focus on hope as I wrote it into my life. It allowed me to paint in words colours I had never seen before in all their raw and glorious honesty: the pain, the beauty, the rebirth of my life.

I could be naked without judgement, open without danger, and writing created an imaginary world of escape where the outcome could be narrated and controlled. It was cathartic and liberating. I craved a sense of normalcy.

While falling pregnant with a child that was not mine may seem a crazy way to achieve this, I had already lost so many of my dreams, and I couldn't bear for this to be stolen too. This challenge offered me purpose and distraction. My life with Lucas had come with so much noise, so much chaos, that without him I felt suddenly plunged into empty space. I lived with rising and familiar panic. My thoughts were disordered, but life had to go on.

It would make me get up, breathe in and out, and move forward with life, overruling any desire to fade into obscurity while I grieved. It was hard; he was everywhere. In things he had left behind: the smell of his aftershave on linen, in the glint of my children's eyes. The places holding our shared history seemed to goad us through the car windows as we passed, invoking nostalgia, and tearing in the fabric of our family.

My focus was also on my children, giving them back their mother and restoring routine, structure, and safety. I talked to the girls about what they wanted. They loved Tereasa; she was part of their family, too, and it had given them joy to be a part of helping achieve motherhood for her. It still felt like the right choice to make.

My world had darkness, but helping others had always been my anchor. I needed it more than ever – something beyond myself to hold on to, a purpose, a guiding presence. I let myself grieve but believed sincerely that good things were ahead. The house was silent. I carried a sleeping Ava, tucking her into bed before climbing into my empty bed.

My husband's moving out began a new dimension of fear. The domestic violence counsellors predicted this, but I could never have prepared for it adequately. It was a cat-and-mouse game he knew how to play far better than I did. But I was learning fast. My heart played tug-of-war for months, still quietly hoping for a miracle. In my mind, I did not believe him anymore. This logic stood steadfast in its reasoning. My body changed direction before my heart could approve the request. But there was no turning back.

'Don't forget, fire burns, Melissa,' were the words he had sent in a text message. These were the words of a man who had lost his power, and this was a battle no one would win. Later, I was chased and almost run off the road by an unknown man in a white Ute. Calling 000, they instructed me to circle a large service station so the cameras would get his registration on camera. For nearly twenty minutes, it continued. Police later informed me the driver was his friend.

I was tracked on social media by my car toll pass. He asked mutual friends for my location, collecting information. There were anonymous letters sent to my employer and the media. Later, a profile with my picture went up on a dating site, and my phone number distributed to random men. It was an incessant chess game, and I constantly awaited his next move. The next battle to protect myself and my daughters had begun.

Some days, I thought about giving up. I was tired of fighting, exhausted from treading water and trying to stay afloat, but it wasn't an option. All that was left was to fight. I knew this man; a decade had given me a solid education on his behaviours and thought patterns. If nothing else, he was predictable. I had almost perfected this juggling act without trying. I slept with one eye open, unable to relax. Emotions surged: anger, fear, sadness, grief, defiance, strength – the injustice of what I was living clawed at me. The fear was a runaway train. If I did not learn to drive it, it would drive me.

13

It was my thirty-third birthday. There was no wine, no parties. The day had coincidently fallen on the day of our first embryo transfer with my own eggs. I drove into Brisbane city meeting Sarah, who shares a birthday.

'Well, happy birthday, ladies,' Dr Buckley teased as he looked up from the notes on his desk and over at Sarah and me, who sat opposite. 'I've got something special for you today,' he continued, his mischievous eyes matching his roguish grin.

'And what might that be?' I asked, shrugging, and nonchalantly playing along. 'I always wanted to get impregnated by a rich, handsome doctor on my birthday… but you'll have to do, I guess,' I retorted, returning fire.

He threw his head back and laughed before narrowing his eyes at me, smiling.

The room was a clinical setting with a bed, benches, and a changing room to the side. His nurse greeted us with a warm smile, giving instructions for me to change into a gown for the transfer. Pulling the curtain closed behind her, she and Sarah stepped out. When they returned, I was sitting on the bed. Sarah squeezed my hand as the doctor returned, meeting my eyes with an expression of half fear, half admiration.

'You know you're fucking crazy, right? I could think of plenty of better things to do on our birthday.' She snorted and shook her head.

I laughed at her bewildered expression.

'Melissa, could you bend your knees, please?' the nurse instructed. 'Now, let your knees fall apart.'

Dr Buckley unwrapped the sterilised equipment while the nurse placed an ultrasound doppler on my stomach. I felt a cold sensation and a tightening down below. In the weeks prior, I'd gone through IVF to create embryos with my eggs and Charles' sperm. Wrinkling my nose from the discomfort, I tried to sit still. It was only a five-minute procedure.

A woman in laboratory clothing came from the room next door. She held a tube, placing it carefully beside the doctor. His movements were methodical as he inserted it into the opening he had made.

A glowing dot floated on the ultrasound screen as I felt a slight twinge in my abdomen. The tight sensation was released shortly after.

'All done,' he announced as he removed his gown and mask.

'You can get dressed now,' the nurse instructed, closing the curtain again.

Pulling on my clothes, it was done. Time would only tell what this day would bring. I was hopeful, but after three difficult miscarriages, it was hard to get my hopes up.

That night, I had a quiet dinner with my children. It was what I needed after a busy week. While life had felt dark, that embryo and its little glowing life inside had become a beacon of hope, something to look forward to. There was so much to live for, even in my darkest hours. I had my beautiful children and incredible friendships.

Placing the cap back on the home pregnancy test, my heart pounded. I watched the fluid line move across the stick, revealing a pink test line in the window and creeping towards the second. It was too early; the transfer had been four days earlier, but I was impatient and dying to know. There was a faint second line, so faint I had to squint.

Holding it up to the bathroom light confirmed it. It was weak, but it was there.

I was pregnant again.

The pregnancy test had been a glimmer of hope and something to hold on for. It was a lighthouse in the storm that was my life and one of the few things sparking passion.

I sent Tereasa a message. 'Hey, what are you up to?'

She replied with an image, a photo of her, her husband, and some friends smiling, holding a glass of wine on Sydney Harbour and dressed in long winter coats.

I replied, sending an image of the pregnancy test with its faint double lines. My phone rang seconds later, Tereasa's name flashing on the screen.

As I answered, she squealed down the phone. 'My God! That's brilliant news, Mel. I'm excited! This time has got to be it.' Her voice was lit with renewed hope and matched how I felt. It didn't make logical sense, but I felt good about things this time. My sensible voice of reason firmly reminded me that getting my hopes up would be unwise.

The days passed by, and I focused on getting up, caring for the kids, and eating at set times of the day because I was pregnant and caring for Tereasa's baby, but otherwise, my focus was simply on not falling apart. I was beginning to rebuild our lives again, learning how to juggle responsibilities as a single parent.

I gained a housemate: Lyndal, a long-time friend, and fellow egg donor, who had moved to Queensland. She was a fiery wild child and yet a wise old soul. A petite, blonde man-eater with an attitude and no filter. Her energy was a welcome distraction and having her around for company on quiet nights was a godsend. Her presence helped fill our empty house.

My friends and family had grown used to the idea and were supportive. I didn't always openly share what I was doing, but if it came up at work or in a conversation, I didn't hide from it. I was secure in my decision and unfazed if people judged my choices. Most people had a limited understanding of surrogacy. It was not an issue regularly featured in the media. So few people underwent the process that it was unlikely those I encountered had ever known anyone involved in surrogacy before.

In my past, short-lived pregnancies, I'd kept a sense of humour as I answered questions people asked, most in awe and overwhelmingly curious but supportive.

'My God, that is disgusting!'

I looked up, shocked at the outburst from a woman who sat opposite me in the staff tearoom. I took in the newspaper headline that had sparked her anger: Australian couple abandons baby boy in Thai surrogacy case.

It had people talking, expressing their views and their justified outrage. I was outraged too but such a complex issue could easily cause separate issues to bleed over the lines, polluting the different colours.

I patted my belly protectively; they had no idea the little life inside was not mine. It had been just over a week since the positive pregnancy test. It was a decision I was proud of, but as I listened to the harsh judgement of others who didn't understand what surrogacy was and tarnished it all with the same brush, it made me reconsider how open I would be to sharing our story.

I read a news article over breakfast and was horrified at the details. David and Wendy Farnell, a Perth couple, had solicited a surrogate in Thailand. After she became pregnant with their twins, they discovered the baby boy, Gammy, had Down syndrome.

The media reported the Farnells returned to Australia without him, taking only his healthy twin sister, Pipah. Gammy had been allegedly abandoned, left in the care of his impoverished surrogate mother in Thailand. This little boy and his story captured the world's attention, highlighting just how complex and fraught commercial surrogacy arrangements can be.

Australians were outraged, and the media was soon filled with stories of other cases gone wrong, adding to the criticism of international commercial surrogacy, and highlighting the problems with Australian law.

Social media overflowed with those expressing their outrage. Some labelled the women who carried a baby for another as 'wombs for rent', suggesting surrogates are forced to carry out of desperation. Others likened it to prostitution.

One of the common questions I got from those who knew I was a surrogate was about payment. Most I spoke to didn't know there was a difference between altruistic surrogacy and overseas commercial options. I was not living in a third world country; I worked and was not living in poverty or forced to do anything against my will. I had signed up because I wanted to do this.

While I usually didn't care what others thought about my life choices, it was hard to dull the noise of criticism on social media, the evening news, and in social conversations. Sometimes I stepped in to educate, sometimes I let it be. My undoing was reading the comments under the published stories.

If people can't have a child, it's God's way of saying they shouldn't.

It's the prostitution of a woman's body.

No one cares about the children; they are a commodity.

What kind of heartless person could give away a child?

My thoughts fell on Tereasa and how she might be taking the controversy and if she would feel judged for her choices. If people knew Tereasa, her warmth, the depth of her pain, and the closeness of our friendship they might understand that we were in this together.

Through the eyes of a newly pregnant surrogate, it seemed few had much understanding of anything. Many of the news articles tarred all intended parents with the same brush as the Farnell's.

I had no fear that Tereasa and Charles would ever leave me with a baby. They had longed for this child for so long, fighting to bring him or her into their lives. There was no mention of the stories of the happy families that resulted or of the voices of the compassionate women volunteering as surrogates to bring these dreams to life.

Tereasa and I set out to offer a positive contrast to the gloom and doom headlines, sharing our story in the media. A contrasting view, another voice. This sparked a sense of injustice in her. The system was so outdated, and laws didn't protect anyone.

Couples who had medical issues that meant they could not carry their babies were not eligible for basic Medicare rebates (despite their conditions often being more serious), unlike those undergoing IVF. Tereasa created a petition, flew to Canberra, and had meetings with a government, that promised an inquiry to examine outdated laws and work towards change. We held together through the negativity.

The little life growing inside mattered, and we willed it on. Turning a destructive news cycle into action and something positive felt like a productive way forward, despite the scrutiny it invited. When the news cycle moved on, people like Tereasa and I would still be here, and it would still be our life.

The early days of pregnancy crept by so slowly I wished them away. Subconsciously, I waited for what sometimes felt inevitable, wondering if fate would offer mercy or give us another blow. It was hard to know whether the time passing would be wasted or count for something. Day by day, the milestones passed, small but significant as life blossomed, entering the world. At seven weeks, a scan revealed a tiny heartbeat, a tiny sac with a tiny foetus. It echoed a familiar song, and I willed it to stay.

By eleven weeks, the heartbeat was strong, like the hooves of a wild horse as its rhythm filled the sonographer's office. We had taken a Harmony test, and all was well. Tereasa and I took the call for results over speakerphone. It revealed her baby was healthy, and my tiny passenger was a girl.

With the news, Tereasa finally allowed herself to dream of her future. I watched her hold tiny, brightly coloured dresses, ribbons, and shoes. She had hesitated before, concerned she might buy baby clothes for a child that would never come. But as she laid her first purchases on the counter at the maternity store and spoke excitedly about impending motherhood, something in her had shifted.

At thirteen weeks, we went for another routine ultrasound. The technician was initially perplexed at the sight of two women, one with a baby bump, the other identifying as Mum, but as we explained our situation, we saw her soften with compassion. She took Tereasa under her wing and once the formalities were complete, she pointed out every detail to Tereasa: her baby's tiny face, toes, fingers, spine, nose. Her eyes glistened with tears; her face filled with wonder. (And I cry as I read this wonderful news.)

I lay back on the table, a sheet covering my middle and my belly exposed, peaceful but silent. I could not take my eyes off her. She had suffered so many losses, five of her own, plus three more I had temporarily carried. Hoping had led to crushing disappointment, yet she was still here. Women are strong and resilient; we can handle more hardship than we ever imagined possible. We soldiered on, moving forward, knowing better days were ahead.

My obstetrician had referred me to see a counsellor when I cried in his office, telling him I struggled to sleep, suffering with anxiety, flashbacks, and panic attacks. Bec was caring, open-minded, and progressive, putting me at ease. She didn't mind how mangled or broken I was, allowing space for whatever memories came up, and the sense of wrongness in my communication that I carried for so long began to dissipate in her presence. She sifted through my broken pieces, seeking out the best of me, holding space for my story. She was easy to talk to; she asked about the surrogacy, my pregnancy, and the stresses in my life. She listened as I unloaded to her, my pain gushing like a torrent. Mostly, I talked about Lucas. How I hated him, how I missed him, how I felt lost, how I felt found, and how to navigate the rat run I found myself in.

He had been messaging me and I was tangled, bound in tiny knots. It felt like a game of cat and mouse. I told her about a message sent just days before: "I miss my wife and our family. I've been thinking about everything, and I want you back. I'll do whatever it takes. I'll always love you."

I exhaled slowly, fiddling with an orange stress ball from her desk.

I switched off my phone and left it, but it got to me, you know? The guilt, the sadness, the memories of the happier times. They still haunt me. Then, the next day, I got another. He told me I'm a stupid bitch and I will regret everything, that I didn't know what he could do, and he would see me in court. It was a quick reality check, but it still hurts.

It felt like the nature of the beast, staying on guard, hypervigilant, because letting down your guard for a moment could cause lasting damage. It was exhausting and I'd had enough.

'To him, it's a game, and the fact I'm still playing means he's winning. Anything we had is so destroyed that I am left deciphering texts that flick between being outright cruel and then loving and remorseful, sometimes one right after the other. It's been months since he left, and the back and forth is exhausting. I think I'm doing well and have moved past the worst things, but then the blackness swallows me up again.'

'So why are you still listening? What more does he need to say?' Bec asked.

I could tell she already knew the answer.

'I don't know. Guilt, shame, sadness, pity?'

'Look at what he is saying,' Bec pressed. 'Even his texts aren't considering what is best for you and don't let you express how you feel or what you need. They are about him. They are about how he feels pain, how he wants his family back, his wife back. He hasn't tried to grasp the pain he has put you all through or expressed how sorry he is. For him, this is about saying what he needs to keep you hooked. He reels you in and casts you out every single day. It's not about you, it's about him.'

I told her, 'You're right.' And she was. Every part of me knew it.

'He told me he's quit smoking, quit drinking, and has joined a men's support program, and he's different now. He knows all the things I want to hear. He says he is on the road to recovery; he gets it. It's so typical of him. He's cured, a changed man before he's even done the work. It's a pattern I know by heart. Instead of giving me time to breathe, to grieve and move on, he keeps me right where he wants me. I've spent so long pondering this. Sometimes, I do so well; other times, I break. But I'm getting better.'

'You are,' Bec replied. 'It's called cognitive dissonance. You led with your heart for a long time, but your head has caught up, and you now recognise his actions and see them for what they are. It takes time for the heart to catch up with the head. But it will. Hang in there.'

I learned to celebrate my friendships, the people who stood by me, holding my head above water when I was drowning in my life. When I took stock of what I was thankful for, the list was long. The choice to be grateful and present didn't come without obstacles but was one I made despite them. Life was not perfect, but it was better.

I often ran on autopilot. I ate because it was required to nourish a growing baby. The baby needed me, and in many ways,

I needed her. We were co-dependent as I attempted to simultaneously feel human and grow a human. The fact she existed prompted me to care for myself, to keep me from falling into a black hole of grief.

At night, as the children went to bed, I felt restless. Leaving Lyndal with the girls, I hit the gym. I felt strong when I put those headphones on with a playlist of angry, girl-power anthems. Steady, moderate exercise and healthy eating did me wonders and was good for my headspace.

I had a healthy glow and slept deeply for the first time in as long as I could remember. Wanting something to look forward to, Sarah and I made plans to travel to Europe after the birth.

Saving for months, I was waiting for the doctor to declare the pregnancy safe, to define a due date. Once we had that, we pulled out travel guides and maps and started planning. She had always wanted to go to Paris, and I wanted to see my sister, who lived in London. We added Rome for the architecture, the culture, and the carbs.

Sarah has always been a history lover, reading about serial killers and world wars. In grade six, while the other children had handed in book reports on middle grade books, Sarah wrote about Jack the Ripper. She was that kid, never outgrowing her curiosity of all things weird. Interested in psychology, human behaviour, and true crime, she added Auschwitz in Poland to our itinerary, and with it came the rest of Eastern and Northern Europe.

Our plans were a guiding star on the days when life felt difficult. Tereasa was there unconditionally, listening and giving spirited pep talks when I was lost. She told me stories of better days ahead, painting my world with hope. I needed something to guide the way.

Pastel balloons danced in the gentle breeze, weaving between the posts of the beachside rotunda nestled in King Edward Park on the Central Coast. Beneath the airy canopy, vibrant sections of fabric adorned the floor, boasting intricate African prints that added a touch of exotic flair to the celebration. The reason for revelry, a poster, 'It's a girl!' hung over the entrance, holding a small gathering of excited women.

In the heart of a spacious, leafy clearing, the dome stood, encircled by dense foliage already shedding its autumnal cloak. The scent of freshly baked cakes mingled with the spray of salt in the air, and the dull thunder of ocean waves against the shore was a soothing backdrop, instilling a profound sense of peace within me.

Families leisurely spread out their picnics on nearby blankets, their gatherings occasionally interrupted by opportunistic seagulls eyeing any scraps left behind. Above, the sky stretched out in a flawless expanse of powder blue, the sun casting its golden rays over the sparkling waters below.

Small groups arrived, bearing brightly wrapped gifts and showering Tereasa with excited greetings and warm hugs. I watched her radiant smile, looking over, gesturing towards me proudly. It's an odd scene to rebuild in my mind, describing how you feel and what it looks like to attend a baby shower of mostly strangers when you're carrying the pregnancy that's being celebrated, but the baby isn't yours. You're an invested spectator, an understudy, a project manager, a prop, defined as a physical element added to a setting for stylistic or emotional effect. The day is not about you, and that's how it should be.

Tereasa seized my hand eagerly, pulling me forward to meet her stepmother, Lynne, and other close family. She had been a tremendous help through the pregnancy and often kept in touch to see how I was. Would they like me? Would they react to my presence, as if I was somehow a threat to their daughter's place as a mother? I needn't have worried. Lynne pushed past the others before her as I approached and scooped me up in a warm and long embrace. Her voice was full of emotion, her eyes teary, telling me, 'You have no idea how much this means to us. Thank you so much for helping bring me my grandchild.'

Her family was warm and kind like Tereasa. I stood back as they chatted and hugged, taking it all in. She was loved by so many, her friends putting so much effort into every detail. A large cake sat in the middle, gift tables were overflowing, and baby shower souvenirs lined the tables. Her friends fussed to make sure everything was perfect. I watched her eyes well with tears as people came to talk to her and express their happiness as her big day had finally come.

As I mingled, introducing myself to other guests as a friend, I noticed changing reactions, slight shock, and glances of admiration.

'Mel, let me introduce you to my friends,' she insisted, linking her arm to mine. The curious eyes of the guests peered at me expectantly, gazing at me as though I were a mystical creature. Patting my baby bump, most gazed at me in admiration, and I could tell others were curious and had questions. How are you going to feel giving up this baby?

Tereasa and I had covered every possible question. There was nothing we couldn't explain or laugh off openly. At the shower was one of my recipient mothers who had recently given birth to a baby boy and had brought him along. Tereasa was instantly in love with the tiny infant. I introduced her to his parents and before long, she cradled him while they disappeared to get a plate of food. Tereasa looked in awe at the little human in her arms. I could almost read her thoughts. *I'm going to be a mum soon.*

'They're going to have trouble getting him back, hey?' I asked her, winking.

She nodded, laughing as she whisked him away to show the other guests. The atmosphere was celebratory. I sat on a deck chair, giving my tired, pregnant body a rest.

I watched her proudly as she opened gifts, admiring tiny dresses, the booties and hats her daughter would someday wear. She gave a heartfelt speech, her eyes welling as she shared our story, and her joy.

Throughout the day, she handed guests brightly coloured pieces of paper, and they sat, looking thoughtful as they wrote. Looking at them quizzically, she read my mind.

'They're doing an activity for later. You'll see,' she added mysteriously. 'You don't get to play because you're the belly. I've got something even better for you.' She handed me a cupcake, laughing.

As we later sat on the grand steps of the dome, packing away the gifts, I saw things in a way I never had before. This pregnancy had touched not just one life but dozens. These people loved her, their presence demonstrating we were not only making a couple parents, but also grandparents, aunts, uncles, and cousins. It was a ripple effect. One action that echoed out, touching the lives of others.

During the latter part of my pregnancy, I had more time on my hands. On maternity leave, my body was tired and swollen but my head was pulsing with nervous activity. I read piles of books, hungry to understand my life, the way I felt, the pain, the triggers, the reasons I had found myself there.

One night, when memories of the fighting and fear were searing and overpowering, I got up from my bed and looked in the bathroom mirror. Seeing my reflection in the mirror, I did not recognise my form. My green eyes were misty, like steam rising off a bitumen road after a rainstorm on a mid-summer's day. My skin was dry and tired. The circles under my eyes were the blue grey of an approaching storm. Pulling my hair into a ponytail, I splashed water on my face, just to feel something. The fear and fury burning within me could not be extinguished or snuffed out.

Sometimes it was so enveloping, burning at my skin, lapping at my lungs that I feared it might cause a shutdown, an overload. Surely the human body was not built for so much sadness. The panic of losing myself, of being pulled under and washed away in a riptide of emotion was frightening. I knew that something had to change, or the weight of the burden would be the end of me.

In that moment, I questioned the limiting patterns I'd subconsciously placed on my life. A story I had written for myself to cope with the pain of being hurt, had caused a knock-on effect. That untrue story, which told me I was undeserving of being loved was now woven into every fibre of my being.

Decades later, the dysfunction and disconnection that defined my childhood reverberated through my life. This, and the wounds from the relationships that followed, lingered like shards of glass embedded in my skin, radiating agony through my body. I tried to cover the damage with a dressing and carry on, but the wound festered, refusing to heal.

There came a time I realised this was untenable. I avoided the idea of greater pain, unable to produce the courage to remedy it. Covering the wound did not make it go away. So finally, I fronted up, ready to begin the journey of excavating it out, of releasing it. I knew it was a process that required courage, vulnerability, and a willingness to confront the pain that had been buried beneath the surface for far too long. I returned to Bec for help unpacking past trauma.

I assumed the sessions would focus on my past relationship, but they stretched far and wide, memories crawling over my skin like an invasive vine, rapacious and noxious. It climbed over me, through me, its spiny arms enveloping me.

Bec held space for me as I recalled my earliest memories, the patchwork of moments making up my childhood. I sat with the little girl I once was, with all her self-loathing, insecurity, and walking on eggshells. Navigating my father's erratic moods had been arduous. He was the forest fire burning out of control, engulfing everything in its path. Then, once in a season, for just a moment, he became the campfire to warm your hands.

My brother, sister, and I would look on with heightened caution, like watching a wild animal. Every interaction with him was calculated, like disarming a ticking time bomb, trying to avoid a catastrophic explosion.

When he rampaged, we tried to stay out of sight while we sat quietly and listened. His arms came down from above like lightning bolts. Trapped underneath, all we could do was watch the storm. During this, my mother remained quiet, never stepping in to shelter us, knowing better than to inflame him while he unleashed lashing words.

The next day, my father spoke as though the previous night had never happened. He would look down on us with soft eyes, though his words were insistent and laced with pain.

'I love you, Miss. You know that, right?' As he floundered, I kept him at arm's length, unable to bear his desperate attempt at mending fences. His words were juxtaposed against the violence weighing us down like a thick and heavy blanket.

I held so much anger. He said I'd be sent to foster care or a girls' home for bad girls like me, while he smashed the few things I cared about. I could not unclench my fists. These memories were so ingrained they were all-encompassing.

As a kid, I'd rarely been able to break through my projection of who my father was to see any of his woundedness. He was supposed to be the grown up. All these things came irrevocably sliding into view, and when I had children of my own, I realised just how much of it was all wrong. As Bec listened on, the unkempt story of my childhood played a cacophony of broken and dysfunctional despair.

I was the sum of all my shitty experiences, my trauma; no longer that little girl but still broken. My father was the first of a long line of men showing me I wasn't worthy, or loveable. I had believed the combined chorus they sang into my life as truth.

I was diagnosed with post-traumatic stress disorder, and I was not ready to hear it. I was afraid of the label; it felt like proof I was irreparably damaged. Labels were shackles, and I had enough of those I'd chained to myself. When this information settled in, it began to bring comfort.

The feelings of intense fear and helplessness, the flashbacks, the horror. Because the memory, in its way, makes you. It becomes a skeleton, a framework for the body of fear and anxiety that follows, something to hang everything else from. It all began to make sense. My mind relived over and over the painful events, the recurring memories. They saturated my senses with vivid images and black nightmares.

I would wake up, unable to move or breathe, frozen by my fear and panic. Trying to run from myself, there was nowhere to hide. My mind raced, constantly wound up and alert. I struggled to sleep, but when I finally did, I slept with one eye open, continually watching for signs of danger, always on guard. I was also emotionally numb and felt detached from everyone around me.

Bec encouraged me to write again, to journal, and to share thoughts and feelings, to let them spill onto the open page as an almost therapy. I did it in secret at first, to disentangle emotions that threatened to strangle me like a noxious climbing vine. The act of picking up a pen felt like taking an axe to the tendrils that spread their spiny fingers around my core. I wrote not to share with others, but to make sense of the disorder and disarray that had spread across my life, creeping up so slowly that I missed it. The mind is mysterious. A master of sleight of hand. I needed to know what else I hadn't noticed.

Things I didn't dare speak anywhere else felt validated as soon as I put pen to page. Secrets weighing like anchors, pulling me down and dragging me under. Things unspoken; the unspeakable ensnared like serrated oyster shells on jagged rocks, secrets tossing me about, tearing up my flesh.

I wrote from a place of isolation, a manmade island, to be free of the acute loneliness entombing me, floating in the open space between my deepest thoughts and ink on page. The liberation felt exhilarating. Like breath becomes air, the words were freedom, flying away from the confines of me. I told stories, giving events narrative, trying to make my memories coherent. These recollections shape a nonlinear narrative, because grief is inherently nonlinear, a voyage that twists and winds, looping over themselves. Two steps forward, one step back.

I took the memories, collecting them like a satin bowerbird: cobalt and sapphire blue pegs, stones, flowers, bottlecaps and feathers to make something beautiful out of the discarded and superfluous. American poet and novelist Sylvia Plath once wrote, 'Perhaps someday I'll crawl back home, beaten, defeated. But not as long as I can make stories out of my heartbreak, beauty out of sorrow.' Perhaps this was the hope that one day this broken thing could be something beautiful.

Most unexpected was what I found in the depths of me. In the cluttered basement and dark cellars were the beliefs, memories, emotions and thoughts stacked in boxes in corners, stories trapped in cobwebs that had gone unnoticed.

Joan Didion once wrote, 'We write to discover what we think', and out of the depths came these truths. Uncovering my voice helped create understanding of my stories that were sometimes beyond my conscious understanding. Things I had pushed down and brushed away came to meet me, to be finally heard. These stories are built on the fallibility of memories, strung together like ropes of pearls.

I wrote into my pain, my hopes, and my joy. I inspected an emotional wasteland, scavenging for treasures or trinkets, beautiful broken things that might salvage meaning from the devastation. I found the willingness to examine and ask questions, to feel and to learn. It's the way you come to find yourself. I had been wounded and bent out of shape, but I was coming back together.

Trauma is a beast that follows you around like a shadow, in the sunshine and the moonlight. It cannot be sent away or silenced, ignored or pushed down. It hunts you, this enigmatic creature, demanding it be heard.

When I drove in the car, I watched the rear-view mirror, taking an alternative route if anyone followed too close. On high alert, I scanned faces like a radar in shopping centres, trying to be invisible. I still moved knives out of sight, checked twice that doors and windows were locked, and drew curtains. Then, the triggers in everyday life snuck up on me when I least expected them. Old places we used to go, people he knew, the smell of lemongrass, a brand of tea, a song playing in the grocery store. These things could set me on fire and burn me down.

When I realised there was an explanation for the physiological responses in my lived experience, it became easier to understand and work through. Like a wound in the flesh, it took treatment and time to heal the invisible scars. It reminded me I was human. I look at it all quite differently now. That day, Bec gave me a map and a destination.

'He loved you the best way he knew how, Mel. He's never had someone to show him what love looks like. It's survival for him, to prove his worth to others, to himself. He can't love you if he doesn't love himself. He tried hard for years; he tried to be someone for you he is not and never will be. You must understand this is not a judgement on whether you are worthy of being loved. You tried your best. You need to accept he is an imperfect, flawed human.'

She shifted in her chair and took a sip from her coffee mug. 'You can't change him. You can control what you do with your life. Who you give your energy, time, and attention to… and you have so many good people in your life. You must know there are bigger and better things for you. It will take time.'

'How much time?'

'I can't tell you. You gave years of your life to someone. You had dreams and hopes for a future together as a couple and a family. You must grieve through it, it's perfectly normal. You will have good days and bad days. You will endure anniversaries, birthdays, Christmas, the children's firsts that you face alone. These will hurt, but you will survive them, and you will be glad you made this choice. Everything will be okay. Hold onto that.'

As the sessions progressed, I began to let go. As she guided me through sitting with the pain and giving it a name, the glass shards that tore me open were released into free air. There was relief, but also a deep feeling of rawness and vulnerability. She told me that eventually the wounds would close, leaving scar tissue, and I would no longer feel the pain. The scars would remain, testament to human strength and resilience, to how much ugliness we could survive.

A huge white moon sat in the night sky when I went driving to be alone, ending up by the lake where Lucas and I had been married. Parking the car, I walked down the stone stairs to the platform by the lake, hearing a symphony of crickets, frogs, and birds. I sat under the lamplight, the glow illuminating the water's edge before the tears fell. I swirled in a tempest of emotion, making the choice to let go of the pain, bitterness, and the regrets that had been weighing me down for so long. I felt a sense of lightness flow over me – a calm amidst the storm. I said goodbye to my marriage and let the memories go, releasing them. The tears dissipated and I felt relief in my bones.

From the warmth of my bed, sunlight beamed in through the curtain edges. My children giggled, cutlery clinked, and Tereasa's cheerful voice sounded from the kitchen. It was Easter Sunday. The aroma of sizzling bacon and freshly ground coffee greeted me as I dragged my pregnant body from bed with an almost sideways roll. As the bedroom door opened, morning light flooded in. Tereasa and Lynne were preparing breakfast, the children looking on. They sat at the kitchen bench eating a chocolate bunny, leaving pieces of foil and chocolate on the tiles.

Sitting at the kitchen table, Charles joined me, holding the morning newspaper. He looked at me with amusement but didn't dare say a word. I probably look like hell, I thought. Tereasa joined us, resting a hot cup of tea where I sat. I smiled gratefully. 'Thank you.'

'Sleep okay?' she asked, pulling a chair beside me.

'I did, thanks,' I answered, sipping my tea. 'How about you?'

'I woke up feeling peaceful and happy,' she said, her eyes twinkling. 'Two days to go now. It feels so close, like it's real.'

I laughed. 'Oh, she's real all right. She has been kicking me from the inside for months. This one is a soccer fan like her dad. We are nearly there.'

The evening before we were due at the hospital, we sat on my king-sized bed, mounds of baby clothes in piles around us, covering the bed. Methodically, Tereasa sorted through each item: the suits, dresses, singlets, shirts, and socks. She pulled a large canvas bag from the floor and filled it with everything she'd need for her baby in the hospital. She touched the delicate materials, marvelling at the tiny size of the baby bonnets. I had seen her this way before; I relished the moment as I watched her. She was daydreaming, perhaps imagining what dressing her daughter might feel like.

I had loved helping bring this baby into Tereasa's world, but I was tired and relieved to have a finish line. There were goals I'd shelved to prioritise this dream. Now, I was ready for the time I could pick them up again. There were things to look forward to.

Sarah and I and the girls would be off on a trip around Europe. After the long, dry spell, I was excited about some adventure and opening a bottle of wine again. Soon enough, this would be a mountain conquered, and I could move on to the next one, whatever that was.

14

From the passenger seat, I looked over at Tereasa as she pulled her black SUV out of the driveway and onto our street. The sky was tinged with hues of pink and orange, the evening air fresh. On the back seat were our maternity bags, side by side. Mine held pyjamas and toiletries, hers, tiny baby clothes and nappies.

Beside the bags was a baby capsule, empty now but awaiting a little passenger. Charles was at home caring for my children. In the Kenyan culture, men do not attend births; it's the role of women. Instead, Lynne had come along to support Tereasa.

Our car arrived and we entered the hospital parking lot, the sunset casting a warm glow over the scene. Tereasa helped me out of the car. Lynne pulled my suitcase as I followed her, shuffling towards the lifts. Sarah was waiting in the lobby, and her eyes lit up when she saw us. Baby photography hung on the walls of the gently lit lobby.

My stomach filled with butterflies; I felt nervous but ready. I was exhausted from pregnancy, but excited about what lay ahead. This journey had taken years, and we were finally approaching the finish line.

A midwife greeted us and showed us to our rooms. We dropped our bags, and I lay down on the bed. The energy in the room was electric. Another midwife entered, checking my observations and preparing to get things started. At 7:30 pm, she began the induction with a hormone called prostaglandin, inducing labour. The dose had its desired effect, and the contractions began in ebbs and flows, before the young midwife could rise from the bedside.

Sarah and Tereasa distracted me with conversation. The contractions grew stronger before dropping away, fading and subsiding. Tereasa rubbed my back in firm, frantic circles as they surged, trying to match my pain with her intensity and sticking faithfully by my side. An hour before midnight, the pain doubled down. On my knees on the bed, the contractions surged through my body, my eyes watering. They moved me to a birth suite, a whitewashed room with a large corner bath, a bed in the centre. A clock hung on the wall. I could hear its faint rhythm over other sounds in the room — the beeping of monitors, the stream of gas. Coloured cords and machines lined my bedside.

'Should we fill up the bath?' Tereasa asked the midwife.

'No, it'll be a while yet. Soon enough,' the midwife assured her. She opened an adjoining bathroom door. 'Perhaps you might want to sit on the ball in the shower. The hot water will do you good,' she suggested gently, handing me two starched, fluffy bath towels, the hospital name embroidered onto each.

The clock read 11:55 pm. 'It's nearly midnight. Go and get a coffee. I'll take a shower,' I insisted, looking at Tereasa. The midwife nodded her agreement.

Sitting on the big blue gym ball, hot water falling from the shower and onto my skin was bliss. As the water rushed down my back, relief came temporarily. I relished it. I wore only underwear; the contractions came and went, but I felt subdued. Grateful for the solitude, I took a moment to collect myself, preparing for what was ahead. The pain continued, overpowering me with each surge. I closed my eyes, counting through it and waiting for it to end. 'Sarah? Sarah! Can you come in and sit with me, please?' I called out as the pain dulled. The door opened, and Sarah slipped in, sitting on a plastic chair opposite me.

'Hey, are you all right?' she asked, her voice gentle and brimming with concern.

'I'm okay. The contractions are getting harder,' I replied, pulling down as I felt another coming. I fell silent, anticipating the pain arriving any second. I cried out, any composure gone. 'Fuck, that hurts.' I winced as it eased.

As another contraction came and went, I leaned back, and there was a strange popping noise and a sensation between my legs. I put my hand down to feel a gush, feeling confused. I met Sarah's eyes.

'Did your waters just break?' she asked, her voice calm.

'I think so,' I replied, desperate for more hot water relief from the shower overhead. 'I'm getting the midwife, Mel,' she insisted, switching off my water.

'Hey, I need that,' I protested, reaching for the handle and switching it on again. Another contraction surged, the pain incredible. The flow of the hot water was the only relief. Within moments, the midwife entered, looking concerned.

'We need to examine you, Mel. You'll need to get out of the shower.'

I had only been in for twenty minutes. As I stood, another contraction surged, bringing tears to my eyes. The pain was almost intolerable.

The young midwife spoke. 'Let's get you something for the pain.'

Oh, thank God.

Tereasa rushed into the room as the midwife fumbled to set up the happy gas, the contractions coming hard and fast. I cried out as the pain came in waves.

The midwife handed me the tube. I gripped it, sucking it in as it rattled, while the pain battered me with each contraction.

Finally, I got lost in the beautiful haze, in a deep pool of blackness and echoes while time stood still. I felt distance from my pain and although I was too exhausted to open my eyes, I heard voices around me, willing me on.

They offered great comfort as moments passed. 'You've got this, Mel. You're doing so well,' Sarah's voice gently urged.

I wilfully inhaled the gas, waves of nausea crashing over me as the contractions surged until my grip on the tube faltered, and my limp hand flopped beside me. The room seemed to echo, everything spinning in slow motion. My cries, primal and raw, emerged from a drugged haze, mingling with the sensation of hot skin stretching and the dull ache of the baby pressing against bone. The urge to push overwhelmed me, but my lips refused to move, leaving me unable to speak. Sarah read my thoughts.

'Do you want to push?' Her voice was an anchor, and I felt her warm touch on my shoulder. I could only nod.

Figures of people in navy scrubs blurred as they moved around the room, their voices isolated and echoing in low tones from far away.

A pretty young midwife sat beside me and instructed, 'Push, push! Well done. Good girl.' With every contraction, the room melted away. Pain burned through every muscle.

An obstetrician appeared at the foot of my bed, but I barely noticed. After a few more minutes of riding contractions, I was in a world of pain, burning. Feeling another contraction and a build-up of pressure, I pushed hard. And like that, the pain was over, and I felt the warm gush of the baby being born between my legs as pressure released.

On my stomach, they lay a warm, gurgling baby letting out a newborn cry. Her eyes were barely open, her body pink, and her head wet, her little fingers curling as she reached out. *Oh, hello*, I thought, in awe. Wow. Look at her.

A wave of relief swept over me. Tereasa stood by my side, tears streaming as she leaned over me, gazing lovingly at her new daughter, gently touching her light caramel skin. She gazed at me with adoring eyes, admiration evident. Sarah and Lynne watched on with awe as I delivered the placenta, and Tereasa cut the cord. The midwife wrapped the tiny baby in a white cloth and handed her to Tereasa. She sat beside my bed, her child nestled against her bare chest, skin to skin.

She beheld her daughter in wonder with an expression of love that melted my heart.

'You're a mum now, you're a mum,' I repeated, my speech still slurred from my drugged state. As reality landed, tears streamed down her cheeks. The baby made gurgling noises, her dark little eyes blinking before they closed again. Her little fingers flexed as they wrapped around her mother's. This was it. This was the moment we had long waited for, worked for, and endured heartache and pain. It had taken sacrifice from both of us, yet it was one of the most magical experiences of my life.

I watched one of my best friends become a mother, and it was an experience I will never forget. The midwife handed me a pump to express milk for the night feeds ahead. I dressed myself and wished Tereasa good night, embracing her tightly. After midnight, I was ready to get some sleep. Tereasa seemed more awake than I had ever seen her, her reality finally better than her dreams. I slept soundly that night, content after watching a little miracle arrive.

'Oh, excuse me. I'm sorry to interrupt.' There was an awkward pause, the midwife's face embarrassed and concerned as she fumbled nervously to leave the room.

'No, no, don't go. You're fine. I'm honestly fine, just emotional.' I laughed, my eyes welling with happy tears.

She appeared confused, insisting, 'I'll come back later,' and shut the door behind her.

Great! I thought. She's going to go back and write notes in the hospital records. 'Surrogate is having emotional difficulties and grieving for her loss after parting with the baby.'

I wasn't, but the emotion of the battle of the last two years had hit me like a freight train, and I was a beautiful mess. Floating in high spirits for days, emotion had peaked. The proud parents had chosen the name Nina. It meant strong.

I held a large, seafoam-green notebook. On the cover were Australian and African animals in water paint, representing the cultures of both parents. Inscribed, 'A new baby is like the beginning of all things: wonder, hope, and the dream of possibilities.' Opening the thick book with its uneven pages, my fingers stroked pages of coloured sheets and photographs glued to each.

There were dozens of letters from people I'd met and perfect strangers: our commonality was that we all loved Tereasa. Each handwritten letter shared a personalised message, explaining what

Nina's birth meant personally to them and how it had changed the lives of Charles and Tereasa. These were the sheets of coloured paper handed out at the baby shower. Now, it all made sense.

Overwhelmed, I read each, one by one. There was a letter from Lynne; I could almost imagine her gentle voice speaking the words. "Dearest Mel, as you read this, please feel the love directed towards you. Sitting in the rotunda at King Edward Park, I am so happy you could be here with some of Tereasa's friends and family. No words can ever express the feelings about the gift, life, and future you have given Tereasa."

Lynne had faithfully supported us through everything. At home, she had cooked for my family when I was heavily pregnant and struggling to attend to domestic tasks. She kept a bedside vigil at Nina's birth, supporting us both. Her words were touching.

Another was from Sarah and a reminder of why I loved her. "You have taught me how to give with an open heart and that it's okay to lose your shit sometimes. That no one is perfect, so why beat yourself up trying? And even when you aren't perfect, and life is falling apart, someone will still love you, warts and all. You've taught me how to find your gift, then give it away, and how the giving brings so much joy into your life. I thank you for that and a million other things every day. You are the most giving, unselfish person I know. When life has knocked you down, you just get back up with a smile and a big fuck you to everyone. I know this surrogacy journey has been hard, and there have been times when you wanted to give up. The way you just kept plodding along, always with the end in sight, is a true testament to your strength and the love you freely give to those closest to you. I'm so proud of you, Mel, you've done it!"

I had done it, and it had been worth every minute.

It was testament to what women can do when they stick together and lift each other up. We are strong and loving creatures, and the kindness and support from women like Sarah, Lynne, and others along the way made it truly unforgettable.

The next letter was from Charles.

"George Bernard Shaw once said, "The reasonable man adapts himself to the world; the unreasonable one persists in trying to adapt the world to himself. Therefore, all progress depends on the unreasonable man." You are truly one of the unreasonable ones, Mel. Over the past few years, as we have come to know each other and have had a shared goal, your determination, persistence, and resilience in the face of some heartbreaking stumbles and falls have been genuinely inspiring. When I seriously considered calling it all off and admitting defeat at one low point, I realised it was no longer just mine and Tereasa's goal. It had also become yours, and you were not ready to give up yet. And so, you had another go. Nine months later, I have fed your kids, and they are safely tucked in bed. You, Tereasa, and the rest of the crew are off to the hospital to deliver a baby girl. You do not know how to quit or admit failure, which is a mighty good thing."

My heart swelled with pride. The night before, in that birth suite, in my drug-induced state, I realised what we had been fighting for had come to fruition.

Tereasa looked at her baby in adoration as her little head rested against her bare chest. Charles arrived at the hospital early the following day to meet his child for the first time. I watched as he sat relaxed, his daughter cradled in his arms: the white muslin wrap a contrast to his dark skin, the colour of ground coffee. Although tiny, Nina already had the beginnings of a wild, dark mane of chocolate curls.

One long chapter had ended, and a new one had begun: parenthood. I turned the book pages, each containing milestones and memories: ultrasounds, home pregnancy tests, bunches of pink balloons for the gender reveal and photographs of our time together. It was our story, a kaleidoscope of love. One of the last letters was the one I treasured most. It was from Tereasa.

"Dear Mel, I always thought I'd be a mum. I started babysitting at nine; people trusted me to look after three kids down the road by the age of twelve. I looked after my nieces throughout high school, which was solidified by coming in the top 2% of the state in my childhood studies. For something most women believe will come naturally to them, becoming a mother has become less of a simple desire and more of the top aspiration – something that has required absolute dedication and hard work from both of us. To say, "I couldn't have done this without you," is an understatement. Becoming a mother brings meaning to my life. It gives me a reason to exist. I have many other important things in my life, but becoming a mother has been my focus for quite a few years now. I am happy this significant goal will be something I get to live now. With this gift you're giving me comes a whole treasure trove of the best gifts I'll always be grateful to you for. Thanks to you, I'll have a Mother's Day. Thanks to you, I can go to an Easter hat parade. Thanks to you, I'll go to birthday parties as someone other than a slightly weird aunt having too much fun with the kids, which will, of course, prompt parents to ask, "Which one is yours?" to which, of course, until now, I've had to uncomfortably reply, "None." Thanks to you, there'll be no more tears at the sight of pregnant women, no more crying at "my lot in life", no more heart-wrenching longing to give my husband the child that would take the two of us from coupledom to the family we have always longed to become. You have made me whole. I will always be grateful for what you've endured for us and intend to repay you by being a good friend to you forever: a loving, caring and loyal friend, just as you have always been to me. It's simple. I will love this gift you've given – the gift of a lifetime of experiences. I know I'll see you in my child and smile. I'll think of your generosity whenever I'm happiest because my heart is bursting with joy at some beautiful new thing the baby has mastered. Thanks to you, I get to hear the word "mummy", and it won't be because a child is so comfortable with me that they've made a mistake, like has happened so many times before. Thanks to you, I get to teach so many things. I get to join a mother's group, I get to breastfeed, I get to make a birthday cake every year, and I get to celebrate Christmas with my child. I have someone who loves me for the rest of my life like no other human can. You've made me whole. You've completed me. I'll thank you today, I'll thank you tomorrow, and I'll thank you for the rest of my life. I love you so much, darling lady. With love, Tereasa."

15

The sun streamed down gently on a damp morning; its warmth on my skin gave me goosebumps, contrasting the chill in the autumn air. The trees shed their brightly coloured leaves. They, like me, had begun the journey of a new beginning, a new life cycle.

It's hard to describe what it feels like when it's over. Beginning again after you've been intertwined in something that consumes your life, I liken it to the feeling of riding a rollercoaster and after it stops, feeling the sensation of hurtling forward as you lie in your bed at night. It takes some time for everything to return to normal, to find your equilibrium.

One of my closest friends was now a mother. Her newborn bundle in an African-print baby wrap pulled close to her body, Tereasa's aura glowed as she adjusted to her new role – the one I knew she was always meant to play.

I wondered if my physical body would look for the child, or I would feel the blues after I gave birth. I made an appointment with Bec as a safeguard, but the days came and went, and I felt nothing but euphoria. The girls and I visited her daily, taking expressed breast milk, meals, a daily newspaper, bread, and coffee to her house. Tereasa had been there for weeks before the birth, cooking and cleaning, doing the school run, caring for me as I carried her child. It had been a team effort, and our team had not disbanded with the birth. Our roles had simply reversed.

Tereasa placed her newborn in my arms. Nina slept, her little lips pressing together, eyelids fluttering, and her fingers curled into a ball beside her cheeks. She was perfect. I was proud.

I felt no bond with Nina, but neither had I felt a strong bond with my children until the days after their birth as I nurtured them. My affinity lay with Tereasa. Through the journey, she had become closer than a sister to me. This tiny baby's life was a testament to our shared determination. A week after Nina was born, Tereasa, Charles, and Nina returned home as a family. We spoke daily via phone and video calls. Tereasa sent photos often.

Their departure cleared way for a new era. What would I do with my life in the whole new world? So much had changed. Emily Dickinson once wrote, 'I am out with lanterns, looking for myself.' This is what I did. I spent time reflecting on my choices, considering how they had led me to where I had been.

I made plans to continue to rebuild my life, making healthy choices for myself and my daughters. I hoped they would grow up with a strong understanding of love and respect in their relationships – that I hadn't left it too late to leave my marriage – and my final acts of courage counted for something. I also reflected on how I could better love myself. In the face of significant ups and downs, I chose to leave the past behind and create a new future.

A few months after Nina was born, Sarah, my daughters and I set off on the trip of a lifetime. We departed for Europe for our joint birthday in July. It was an adventure we had waited for, celebrating milestones for each of us.

It was Sarah's first trip overseas, and she had a fear of flying.

She gripped her armrest, knuckles white and high on Valium, and the flight took off as I held her hand.

Our trip was a whirlwind journey. After almost a year of sobriety, I made up for lost time. We danced in toga costumes in Rome, downing cocktails in small buckets. We sampled copious amounts of French champagne available at every corner store.

As we caught planes, buses, and trains through Europe, I soaked up every moment. I wrote in journals and read novels as we travelled. I took time to plan, dream, and contemplate.

Something clicked, and I was ready to pick up the pieces and move on with my life. I was still broken with heart scars that would take time to heal, but I was ready to face the future headfirst. Peace came from acceptance. I can't pinpoint the moment I found it, but to realise it was there was beautiful. I understood life was to be embraced rather than endured; each day wasn't a stepping stone closer to happiness as a destination. What I was looking for was found on the journey, these moments with my beautiful children, my friendships, and the times we shared. This was life.

I celebrated the friends and family who loved me and lifted me when I fell, and the good men who reminded me I was worth loving and gave me hope. I even acquired gratitude for my foes: those who made me bleed. They brought me to my knees but taught me to look up at the endless sky, teaching valuable lessons about love, life, and most importantly, myself.

I was finally at a place of happiness and gratitude, chasing ambitions without being held back and no longer needing the validation of another to see my worth. It was liberating.

My daughters visited their aunt and cousins in London while Sarah and I toured Eastern Europe. Arriving back in London, we caught the Eurostar to Paris. With a little over a week to go before we returned home to Australia, our holiday was almost over.

That evening we sat on blankets on the Parc du Champ de Mars, the lawn below the Eiffel Tower. Barefoot, we arranged plastic champagne glasses, and a basket of goods purchased from a deli below our apartment. Behind us, the magnificent landmark twinkled in contrast to the night sky, lighting the park and leaving us speechless with wonder.

Sarah handed me a glass of champagne, its fruity-floral scent delightful to my senses. We sat back, taking a minute to breathe in every magical moment and the beauty of what was around us.

'Hello, Paris,' I murmured in wonder, aloud to no one in particular.

'It's beautiful, isn't it?' whispered Sarah.

I could only nod. As the girls cartwheeled on the grass, we watched people move about their bustling lives. We were intercepted by a small group of gypsy men with dreadlocks, jingling handfuls of coloured metallic key rings in the tower's shape. 'Three for one euro,' they hollered, swarming in on anyone who responded with eye contact.

'I found you a nice French boyfriend, Mel,' Sarah joked, pointing to a young man who was busy hustling an American tourist nearby.

I laughed. 'Thanks. With all these strapping young men, there's still time to tick off a bucket list item for you, too.'

'Kissing the love of my life under the Eiffel Tower?'

'Yep. That's the one.'

'Sure, I can do that,' she answered dryly, a twinkle of amusement in her eye. 'One day, we will come back here with the loves of our lives.'

'We will,' I replied, reaching to pour more champagne. I

handed one to her, and she accepted it gratefully. We clinked the plastic glasses.

'To the future and ticking many more adventures off our bucket lists.'

The stone stairs of the old library were dusty, and the falling leaves of autumn patterned the path ahead in shades of red, orange, and yellow. The street nearby was quiet, with only the sound of a distant lawn mower and occasional passing cars breaking the silence. I was early, giving myself time to digest what I was doing there.

I had taken some time away to travel and breathe. Now I was home again; my trip had done my soul a world of good. I felt the pain subsiding, the grief and anger evaporating through my skin. I was ready to move on, and this was the next step.

Climbing the old stone stairs, I opened a solid glass door and entered an open foyer. An A-frame sign on the dark carpet spelled 'Pathways', vague wording with an arrow pointing to a small room down the hall. Approaching the doorway, a woman looked up and smiled like she'd been expecting me.

'Hi,' she said brightly. 'Are you here for the group?'

I hesitated. 'Yes, I am.' I gulped, trying to keep a handle on my nerves. Seeming to sense this, she took control, directing me inside. Eleven women sat around a large table. Casually dressed, many wore jeans and track pants, sweaters, and coats. A couple of the ladies held babies, their prams parked beside the table. The women's ages ranged from the early twenties up to mid-fifties. They chatted among themselves and sipped coffee, acknowledging me with a smile as I sat. What was I doing here?

The week prior, I had spoken with Hannah. 'I'd like you to consider joining the group, Mel. Lots of people benefit from it.

You will, too,' she said.

I agreed willingly, trusting her judgement. And there I was.

I looked around at the women, feeling out of place. 'I don't belong here,' screamed an internal voice, urging me to run. A woman closed the room door and stepped up to the table.

'Hi, I'm Jen,' she spoke, her voice calm. 'I'm your group leader. Welcome to our program. We are here to support and help those of you who have been through violence to understand your situation better. To understand how to recognise the signs and identify the behaviours and patterns.' She put a book down on the desk in front of her, taking a seat.

'Can we introduce ourselves to the group? If you feel comfortable, please share a little about what's brought you here?' She gently placed her hand on the shoulder of a short redhead girl beside her. 'Ariel? Would you like to begin?'

Ariel nodded, clearing her throat as she found the courage to speak.

'I'm Ariel. I'm not even sure why I'm here. I guess it's because I still feel lost. I'm trying to get my life back to normal again, and I thought it would be easier by now. I left my partner eleven months ago with my son. It got gradually worse for us. He was insecure and wanted to know where I was all the time. He shoved me against the walls and called me a slut. One day, I asked a waiter at a restaurant for something for my son, and he accused me of cheating on him, punching me in the eye while I was holding my son. I couldn't do it anymore. So here I am.' She shrugged, her head down.

'Thank you, Ariel,' Jen encouraged her.

I glanced at Ariel, who was quiet. My heart hurt for her.

'Julia?' Jen spoke to the girl sitting beside her.

Julia appeared in her early forties and was dressed impeccably.

'Hi, I've been separated from my husband for two years. He never hit me but was quite controlling.' She paused. 'He watched every cent I spent. He was furious when I spent time with my family and friends. He would get people to check on me and scream at me and the kids. It was like walking on eggshells. I looked at my daughter; she was ten. I wondered if this behaviour would repeat itself in the future. Would she marry a man like her father because it was all she knew? She stayed in her room, hiding from his temper. It was no quality of life.' Julia traced her fingers across the lines of the table as if studying its every detail, then continued, 'Then, one day, something changed. My teenaged son began abusing his sister as my husband had done to me. When I left, my husband closed all our business accounts and drained our money. He refuses to pay child support and still sends abusive messages. I want to find ways to cope with and understand this. Thanks.'

The eyes of the other women were fixed on her every word, nodding as she finished. As each woman spoke, I watched them intently, feeling great empathy for their stories. Then, their eyes turned to me.

'I'm Mel. I've been separated from my husband since the middle of 2014, almost a year now. I'm getting better, but I still feel broken, and I can't be that way anymore. I want a better life for me and my daughters.'

I continued, meeting Julia's eye with a knowing look.

'If they grew up to marry a man like their father or thought what we went through was normal, I don't think I could forgive myself. When I left, I knew although I loved him, we could not live like that anymore. I wanted my life back. I have now moved on in life and am trying to find my way again and be at peace with myself.

Peace is what I want more than anything. I want to understand the past for a better future, so I don't repeat past mistakes. Thanks for listening.'

I sat, emotional, as the next woman took her turn to speak. I'd heard the words from my mouth, and somehow, they even surprised me. I then realised something important. I was wrong. I did belong here. We were all different kinds of the same.

These women challenged the stereotypes of what and who could be a domestic violence victim. There were so many myths. Weak, uneducated, dependent, lacking confidence, ambition, and self-worth. But these women were from different walks of life and were none of those things.

I attended the workshops week after week. I had started with plenty of 'what', and now I needed the 'why'. I began to see old truths in a new light. In the years of crisis counselling, I saw graphs and diagrams. I knew I was a broken woman, and the chances of him changing were almost zero, but I was in denial. There were a few lessons that caught my attention, naming something I had felt for a long time. White Knight Syndrome.

Jen said that people with White Knight Syndrome are rescuers, often women, who feel pulled to rescue people in relationships, even at the expense of their own needs or wellbeing. In their eyes, they see those they rescue as damaged or vulnerable.

She explained that women who are often socially conditioned to take on the role of nurturer, may be more likely to be drawn to partners who have addictions, patterns of abusive behaviour, or infidelity issues. Rather than finding partners where the relationship is equal, where there is true intimacy, and both partners are emotionally fulfilled, they seek out unhealthy partners who seem to need them. By doing this, they avoid focusing on healing themselves. They may be empathetic to the point of denial, denying their partners have self-control over their behaviour, making excuses and hiding their behaviours from others to protect them. This shields them from consequences or accountability.

The sheer force of the relief I felt about understanding this mysterious state I'd existed in caught me off guard, put me off balance.

White Knight Syndrome. The Rescuer. The Fixer. All of these were me.

Jen continued to explain that those who are most likely to have these characteristics are people who have themselves been through abandonment or abuse from their caregivers, their parents. They may have a history of trauma. Since no one came to rescue them, they become the rescuers. I realised all of this was me.

This single revelation followed me around for days. I had been searching for a destination, and Jen had just handed me a map. Looking back on what I had learned, I realised I had a type. There was certainly a pattern. I fell in love with broken men, ones I thought needed rescuing. Drawn to the bird with the broken wing, my immediate instinct was to rescue and nurse these wounded creatures back to health.

The next session shone a light on parenting patterns tied to children with higher rates of domestic violence. Those who grew up in angry, abusive, violent, neglectful, or distant households were more likely to accept the same for themselves in future relationships. I understood the correlation for myself in my upbringing but also contemplated how it might impact my daughters' experiences. The thought terrified me.

Being a good mum would not stop my daughters from feeling pain and my trying to save everyone else would not save me. I stayed for so long, martyring myself to avoid being responsible for my children growing up without a father.

I looked at the same diagrams with new eyes. I learned to understand what domestic violence is, what led to its beginning and how to avoid making the same mistake in future relationships. My greatest fear was that I would repeat old patterns only to end up back on the same road. I finally understood the 'why'.

Time passed and I found the courage to be open about my story in hopes it might resonate with even one person going through the same. Of the many thousands of words I have published about a variety of topics, this is one I kept secret. Somehow it felt less real, less shameful if hidden away and not exposed to air or light.

Almost every woman I encountered had her own story to tell. Cautiously or fearlessly, she shared a traumatic experience of her life or of someone close to her. During these moments, I realised how little public conversation occurred around something that was reality for so many women. The fact I wasn't alone was both comforting and painful, but it stirred a sense of injustice in me, a simmer, a flicker of flame in the ashes. I could not promise justice would prevail or sell them a dream of a fairytale ending. I could not promise a peaceful, sunny existence. But I found victims identified more with real pain than with platitudes.

However, just because you think you are done with the past doesn't always mean the past is done with you.

Court proceedings began, and with it, he found a new way to abuse me. A campaign of character assassination, the legal system was a weapon used against me. Fighting in the courts was like inflicting hundreds of papercuts. It reopened old wounds, forcing me to relive my trauma all over again. Any pretence of moving on was submerged in deep water.

At first, letters arriving from his lawyer were sharp, sudden, and piercing. They hit my psyche like a drive-by shooting. I dangled from the edge, not knowing how to protect myself. Feeling ill-equipped, helpless, and scared, I made the decision I would not fall.

I read websites, textbooks, and legislation until the early hours. I devoured and memorised any information that might help save us. Using the information to represent myself in court, I began a law degree and was determined I would not spend my savings fighting him. I visited legal centres and sat before dozens of community lawyers, gathering information – tools and weapons to protect myself, fashioning makeshift armour out of knowledge to survive.

My kitchen table held mountains of paperwork: affidavits, restraining orders, hospital records, child safety documents, letters and records from counsellors and the domestic violence centres and hotlines.

I began to string words together like beads to tell a story, desperate to adequately communicate the fear, to paint a picture of years of anguish, and sew together a patchwork of bruised flesh, blood-stained pyjamas, smashed furnishings, words that tore, fear that froze, guilt that punctured, and the promises broken.

I sat down one day when the kids went off to school, ready to relive it, to feel everything, and dive deep into the places I had closed off to survive. Images and ghosts from the past flashed back as I wrote.

I revisited myself on a hospital bed, having my face stitched back together, checking in at friends' places and hotels late at night because I was frightened; the nights, the fights, and the crossed lines I had never found salvation for. I felt sick and overwhelmed. Fanged spiders crawled out of dark corners. The closed doors of the abandoned rooms of my mind I'd left unmoved for so long were pulled open, jars of unpleasant memories I had stored away were uncapped.

There was no way the task could be consumed in bite-sized pieces, a little each day. There was no time to lick my wounds. I had to consume it all at once, to meet the pain so it could all be over. I read the records, page by page, including the observations of various counsellors who had quoted our conversations over the years in their notes. Looking back, I'm amazed by what I read, both by the jarring reality of their assessments of me and by the strength I showed in my vulnerability. To admit to fear and uncertainty felt like a sign of weakness. But there was a boldness in the words recorded there I had refused to edit in my angst and fear. The words emerging were raw and honest. My salvation came in the moments I broke.

It's strange to understand how we give those we love so much power over us. I had allowed him to shape my own definition of myself, to devalue my self-worth. There is no greater power than that.

As I sat at the table and read, I offered myself an act of love by reaching down to my past self, pulling her up and teaching her how to crawl, and then to walk again. I went in and out of court, my life scrutinised and tethered. The legal challenges were another battle to fight, and laying down my sword was never an option.

Fear and hope spurred me forward as I realised at a time when I should have been protected, that I would have to stand up and fight. I was ready.

I pitied Lucas and spent my adult life protecting him from

himself and the opposing views of others. I had believed he was sorry and in pain because he had lost us. But his court affidavits revealed none of my beliefs were true. Memories returned of the time he had smashed my laptop. He seemed sorry. Now, in black and white was confirmation he didn't.

"Melissa stated that the laptop was hers. However, this is untrue. The laptop belonged to me. I smashed it as I was sick and tired of the time Melissa spent on it."

When he had punched me, and I needed stitches to my face, it had been one of the worst nights of my life. It left scars both physically and psychologically. His response minimised it like it meant nothing. He had no idea it had almost destroyed me.

"I did cause serious injury to Melissa's lip, but it wasn't to cause her pain. I admit I probably pushed her harder than I intended, as the force of my body against hers caused her to fall onto the edge of the wall and cut her lip. I was shocked and upset to see the injury to her lip. Melissa was screaming and carrying on."

Carrying on. Is that what someone does when bleeding, in pain, and can touch their teeth through their broken face?

When explaining the incident when he punched me in Chiang Mai, he wrote:"

I was angry at this point and pushed my arms out to shove her away, hitting her square in the nose with the base of my palm. Melissa fell onto the ground, crying and shouting at me. There was a lot of blood. I tried to help her clean up, but she wouldn't let me near her. Her brother Robert came into the room as he heard the commotion. He saw Melissa and then went and removed our youngest daughter from the room. I felt humiliated about what had happened, but at the same time, I was angry and frustrated about why the incident had even occurred in the first place."

Comment after comment showed he believed he was a victim of a system, of society, and me. None of it was his fault. It was all just an accident – an uncomfortable, unfortunate misunderstanding.

"'I admit there were times when I accidentally caused physical harm to Melissa. These were never out of anger or aggression, though. As a split-second reaction, I put my hand out to shove her away and got her in the eye. I felt bad for what had happened, but Melissa made out like I was the worst person in the world for hurting her, yet there was never any remorse for what she did to me."

Accidentally? If any part of me believed he was sorry for what he'd done, it was gone now. Any remaining positive memories of him felt corrupt, based heavily on misconception. Reading his words ripped me open all over again. On those days in court and the weeks beyond, those memories circled my head, clouding my view like a flock of seagulls rushing in for a single morsel of bread. I could not see clearly. I felt too much of everything.

The Domestic Violence Support Services were a godsend, reaching down and pulling me up from the murky depths, breathing hope into me when I was drowning in despair. I'm not sure what I would have done without them there to catch me, perhaps chewing off my limbs, like a wolf caught in a trap – destroying myself in the struggle to get away.

They could offer a listening ear or access to a refuge on the other side of the state. There was no silver bullet. The more I looked for help, for a detail, a loophole to save us, the more I realised society was not adequately prepared to deal with such an issue. We are outgunned, not just by abusers, but by poor public education, inadequate government legislation, insufficient funding;

navigating it in real time was like one person trying to hold back a changing tide.

That year, 2015, was a year when family violence filled the headlines, and the issue was an epidemic, with almost two women killed every week: 103 women were killed in family and domestic violence-related homicides that year. Politicians stood in front of television cameras, their faces severe and sympathetic as they spoke about the women being murdered by the men who were supposed to love them. They made promises and delivered delicately crafted speeches to show they cared before they turned around and didn't.

In writing this, I use an alias for my abuser, but in reality, it doesn't really matter. To find the extent of this issue, all you have to do is open a newspaper, social media or to scroll through the daily news. As I sit here and write this, I would love to tell you that in the years past that everything has changed, but that would be an untruth. This year, a woman has been killed by family and domestic violence, on average, every four days. The endemic remains, as we count the victims of the hands of other humans, but also a defective system.

A sense of injustice transformed my being, lingering, and spurring me to do something. I understood this incredible energy had risen from my anger and grief. Either I could harness and ride it, or it would drive me. So, I took control.

During this time, I met Dani, a young English woman who became a friend and confidant. She, too, had been the victim of an abusive partner. There were many things that never had to be translated between us. She understood. I saw her fear and pain. But most of all, I saw her strength. She was a survivor.

She had fled to a new state to escape her ex-partner and begin a new life. He tracked her down again, and her fight continued. She shared the sense of injustice and defiance I felt. It was an era when the topic was on everyone's lips. It was a staple in the media. Several women died each week, and Rosie Batty was Australian of the Year, a beacon of light fighting for change alongside us. I remembered watching her speak with such conviction and strength, the saddest smiling woman I had ever seen. I wondered how she could carry the weight of grief. Her words were hope, like a lantern swinging in the dark for so many of us. A friendship blossomed between Dani and I; we were a force to be reckoned with.

We campaigned for change in family violence and the law, writing to politicians, launching online petitions, and speaking out through media stories. People could empathise with real people, and this was our life. If just one person read our stories and saw something they recognised about their own lives in ours, feeling compelled to act, it was worth it. We channelled rage at injustice into the fire, determined to make something beautiful out of the ashes in our dark reminiscence, in hope that what burns hottest may light the way.

We were relentless in the pursuit of a revolution. Things had to be different; things would be different. We sat in Queensland Parliament with Premier Annastacia Palaszczuk and other elected members, pressing for a review of laws affecting family violence victims. We presented a petition with nearly one hundred thousand signatures. The government brought forward the legislation, and the laws passed. The pain spurred me to pursue this, and a sense of injustice burned me. I caught fire. When faced with fight-or-flight, I chose to fight.

The court proceedings with Lucas went on for two years, and they weren't severable from the rest of my life. Once the blaze of anger in me passed, I found peace. It wasn't easy, but eventually, I chose to let go, to trust and have faith. The legal fighting stopped inhibiting my joy the way it had initially. I became more defiant and less angry. I was ready to move forward.

One evening, after filing for divorce, I sat drinking champagne, wearing a plastic tiara, laughing as I fed a small bonfire in my yard. I burned our wedding photos and his suit, the letters and cards he had given me over the years of the relationship, things I hadn't been ready to let go of. It was liberating.

I cleaned out my closets, in a life spring clean, to eliminate anything that was tainted with memories of the past. I wanted to lay to rest the old me, to pull up the roots of anything that didn't belong. There were moments I hesitated.

I called my sister Elle when I came across Lizzie, the porcelain doll I had owned for nearly three decades. Her legs were smashed by my father's temper decades earlier, and every time I looked at her, the feeling was bittersweet. She was a reminder of my nanna's love but more a reminder of anger and fear of my father's actions that I wanted erased from my life — every trace of it. The metamorphosis had begun.

Despite the hard times, I chose to make the most of the days I had. I did not want to come out the other side of the battle and have only existed through those days. I would not let Lucas ~~him~~ take any more than I had already given. Deep in my veins, I also believed karma comes without our help, that he would destroy himself with his own actions.

The day finally came. It was the day he took the stand in a contested hearing that would decide our future. I told myself to breathe. Breathe in, breathe out. Sit up straight and speak clearly.

Don't make eye contact. Stay calm. My lawyers were a comfort but made no promises; they gave no assurances that things would be fine – expectation management.

Lucas was the first to take the stand when the court was brought into session. He wore a suit, had shaved, and tried to be on his best behaviour. Looking smug on the stand, we sat waiting for the day to begin. As he met my eye, I saw hatred. He was the predator, and the hunt had begun.

One hour into cross-examination, Lucas was caught lying under oath and rebuked repeatedly by the judge for refusing to answer questions. I watched the judge, his body language telling me everything I needed to know. When he declared a break, he rose from his seat, spun his black robe and slammed the chamber door behind him. I saw Lucas's barrister shift uncomfortably and raise his hand to his forehead. I tasted blood.

Some people unravel under pressure, and I watched as Lucas picked himself apart. He could not keep up the pretence. He was both his team's most significant liability and our biggest asset.

My barrister grilled him about the violence, exposing his vulnerabilities and going for the jugular. Lucas argued, revealing his combative and snarky side. He spent a long time appearing to contemplate questions without giving answers, and when he did, he fumbled and fell.

'Do you know what domestic violence is, sir?' my barrister questioned him.

'It's when you hurt or kill someone you're in a relationship with?'

'Yes, that's a start. What about tracking a partner's movements? Calling them a slut? What about smashing items in their household? Have you ever smashed or broken any household items, sir?'

'Maybe, a few things. A laptop. But it was my laptop, and I had the right to smash it if I wanted to,' he answered with a slight smirk.

'Don't you think that behaviour might cause her fear?' the barrister asked calmly, pausing for impact.

'No. I don't think so.' Lucas stared him down but now seemed unsure if he was the hunter or the prey.

I sat innocuously behind my lawyer, giving nothing away in my facial expression. The judge sat back in his chair, head back, arms crossed tightly across his chest. His eyes were closed, his face tight, visibly incensed.

The barrister then asked about the incident in the Chiang Mai hotel room. Lucas agreed it had occurred and conceded there had been a little bit of blood. The barrister jumped on his answer, scooping up his affidavit and pulling open the pages. 'Sir, you wrote in an affidavit there was A LOT of blood. Which version wasn't truthful?'

'Ummm.' Lucas fumbled, seemingly considering the consequences of each answer. My barrister grilled him again.

'You either lied in your testimony moments ago or were dishonest in your affidavit. Which is it?' His voice was clear and firm. The room was dead silent as Lucas contemplated his answer, stealing looks at his lawyer, reaching out silently for help.

'My testimony right now was wrong,' he finally offered.

The barrister moved quickly, keeping the momentum going. Pressing Lucas more about the injury to my face. His responses were vague, explaining he had gently pushed me on the front of my body, and I spun around like a ballerina doing a pirouette and hit the wall. He claimed it was all just an accident.

I sat quietly on the court bench, trying to keep it together as my eyes teared up. I kept my eyes on the ground but saw His Honour looking at me, noting my emotional response to Lucas's testimony as I relived history in that courtroom.

The judge sprang to life, finally having had enough of all he had heard. 'So that is your testimony, sir? I remind you, you are under oath. That is the version you are swearing to in this court?' His voice was jagged with sharp edges, and his face lit up like an approaching thunderstorm.

'Yes.' Lucas nodded.

The judge leaned forward, looking angry. 'That is absolutely ridiculous.'

Lucas's barrister stood quickly. 'Your honour, I have to object to ridiculous.'

'Sit down!' His Honour barked back. 'I will be noting it in my judgement. Your client has been sitting here for hours with no signs of honesty or taking responsibility for his actions. In my twenty-six years as a Crown prosecutor, I have never heard such a ridiculous explanation for violence. None of it makes any sense. It defies any sense of logic; no reasonable person would believe what he says. Your client must think I'm a total fool.' He shook his head angrily.

My barrister continued questioning Lucas about events in our history, pressing him for answers, under oath, to some difficult questions. What Lucas had sought to keep hidden had been dragged into the light, and he had driven himself from the road.

I felt validated and heard for the first time in those proceedings. It opened my cage to reveal an endless blue sky in every direction. I had always hoped Lucas might one day apologise. But that day, I realised it would never happen and accepted that. I no longer wanted or needed it.

After Lucas stepped down, I gave my testimony. I prepared to get ripped apart by the barristers on the other side. I answered the questions they asked and stepped down from the stand. Over the next day, court-appointed experts stepped up to testify.

I let it all go. The outcome was in the stars; I had to let it play out. Either way, there would be an answer, and I could get on with my life. There would be closure for all of us.

The verdict took a couple of weeks to come back. It came suddenly and unexpectedly on a day we appeared to attend to another matter. The judge mercifully gave me back my life and our freedom.

Part of the judgement read: The mother details many instances of domestic violence in her affidavit, and I don't have to delve into the particulars of those allegations. However, there are two instances which do illustrate the attitude of both the mother and father in this regard. The first occurred on 28 December 2008. The mother claims she and the father were arguing, and she realised she should get herself and the children out of the immediate vicinity. She said she grabbed a few items, began to leave and tried to call the police. Lily, who was five years old at the time, was hiding behind her and crying as the father screamed at the mother. The mother picked up Ava, who was ten months old at the time, as she moved towards the front door to leave. The mother claims the father then shoved her against the wall near the front door, and then, after a struggle, he punched her in the face, splitting her teeth through her face and upper lip. She said she bled severely and was hysterical. She took the girls outside of their house to sit on the front lawn and noted that Lily was vomiting because of the distress. She claims the father came out to the lawn, kneeled, sobbing, and apologised over and over. The mother had called the police and told the father that the police were coming. He appeared to panic and begged her to get into a car and that he would take her to the hospital before the police arrived. This ultimately occurred, and on the way to the hospital, the mother phoned the police to say that she was going to the hospital. In his evidence before me, the father gave an absolutely ridiculous explanation as to what he said occurred on this occasion. He claimed that the mother was the one who was assaulting him and that he was covering himself to avoid her punches. In a move of self-defence, he then pushed her but was not watching what he was doing. When he looked, he realised that his push had caused the mother to go face-first into a door corner, which split her lip. He said he was extremely sorry for this.

The mechanism described by the husband is inherently incredible. He claims to have pushed a woman who was punching him. The force that he applied to her body must have been to the front of her body, yet this is the part of her that is injured. He tried to say that the force of his push may have spun her around in such a way that made her face then hit the area of the wall that he said that it hit. The father's explanation is illogical, and I find it dishonest. No reasonable person could ever accept the explanation given by the father.

The second incident occurred in November 2012 when the mother and father were holidaying in Chiang Mai in Thailand. Other members of the mother's family were there as well. The mother says that the father went out drinking, and when he returned, they argued. The mother says that she was in some way blocking his entrance to the room, but he shoved her out of the way. She said that she became upset and angry and told him that he shouldn't touch her, and she then pushed him back. She claims the father then punched her hard in the face, knocking her back against the wall. She says she fell to the ground, and her nose was bleeding very badly, leaving a pool of blood on the floor. Ava, who was nearly five at this time, had woken up. The mother's brother came into the room and took Ava out of the room. The explanation of the father for this incident was that the mother was the one who was assaulting him, and he was covering himself to protect himself from her blows. He then pushed out to get her off and accidentally struck her with the palm of his hand, and this blow with the palm of his hand was what caused her nose to bleed. Again, I find this explanation inherently incredible.

The father lacks insight into his domestically violent behaviour and will not acknowledge his role in what has occurred. Having had these two incidents explained to me in evidence in such a dishonest way by the father, I am inclined to accept the evidence of the mother that there was far more domestically violent behaviour by the father than he is prepared to admit. The father has shown no remorse for what he has done, and despite the submissions of his counsel, he has not taken true responsibility for his behaviour. He has minimised these incidents of domestic violence and attempted to paint a picture that there has simply been an unfortunate series of accidents that have occurred in the course of the relationship.

For years, I had carried unpacked baggage, and then, one day, it was over. I walked out of the court free and into the rest of my life. Slowly, Lucas faded into the background, his presence shrinking until it was nothing more than a memory. With his power broken, I felt peace, the weight lifted from my shoulders. He met a new girl and I saw my old self in her reflection, a nurturer cradling a bird with a broken wing. I hope that in his next life he is kind to her, that all the brokenness made him a better man.

It made me strong and resilient. I used my experience to campaign for law reform for those suffering from family violence. It was liberating. I found my voice. In this, I found my reason why. For anyone who can identify with my story or the stories in this book of others' hardships, I want you to know there is life beyond your struggle.

16

The sun began to descend, its glare fading, the sky golden. There were shades of pinks and purples throughout the powdery blue, a child's finger painting on the skyline. I could taste the ocean salt and felt the grains of sand beneath my toes. I'd longed to dip my feet in the ocean, packing up the car, and journeying here, a short pilgrimage to where I felt I could breathe again.

My daughters twirled their dresses and did cartwheels, letting out squeals of rapture, their figures tiny dancing silhouettes on the golden sand. I watched in awe from my beach towel; my hair still wet from the ocean. There was no one else for miles, except an older man in the distance throwing driftwood for his collie, its bounding body leaping into the surf to retrieve it.

I listened to the crash of the waves and watched gulls diving into the shallows. My children followed, and the water greeted their ankles as they plunged into the lagoon pools near the shore, laughing as they splashed.

I had never gone away, but how I had missed them.

While there physically, I was not always present: lost, buried, and sinking in quicksand of hurt. Broken in every way, I was a shell of my former self, with brittle bones, battle scars, and a desperation to feel good enough. I saw the scars on my face, and they represented the brokenness I felt inside. There's a quiet sadness I feel will never completely disappear, absorbed like sound and light. The existence of these scars, their raised tissue, felt like proof I had been unloved by my father and by Lucas. But also, by me.

Those scars took me back in time when I looked into the mirror. They felt like a branding, a marker, like somebody owned me. What followed was obsession with making them disappear.

I bought the best make-up and visited skin clinics to ask if they could fill the valleys of the tissue with needling or injectables. I consulted with plastic surgeons to see if they had a treatment that could fix all the broken parts of me. As they prodded at the scar lines given to me by the men who were supposed to love me, each asked how they got there. Again, I went back in time.

I had seen Bec a few days earlier, feeling defeated as I told her of my quest to erase the past, to pull together the broken parts. Those I had seen had assessed me and decided there was little they could do, that these scars of mine were not going away.

Bec listened and then said something profound.

'Mel, life is full of scars. These are the result of things you have endured and survived. They are the result of the things you have attempted or accomplished. The fearless part of you.

'You have beautiful stretch marks from your growing belly, fading now but proof of the battles you won. You carried them, and played a part of the miracle of creation, not just for your children but for others. You have fallen and got up again. You have suffered loss, pain, hardship, and shown resilience to overcome all life threw at you. What if you reframed your scars like this?'

I looked at her, perplexed at this new idea. She continued, 'What if those scars are a road map of your story? What if they symbolised your strength and resilience, of all you have overcome?'

She paused for a moment, typing on her computer. Seconds later, she turned the screen around to show me a picture. It was an image of a beautiful piece of pottery with gold lines across the surfaces.

'In Japan, broken pottery is repaired with valuable metals in the art of Kintsugi; the Japanese call it the art of precious scars. They use the metals to repair the broken pottery, which makes the scars more prominent, thus enhancing their beauty. The repaired item now takes on a new life and is even more treasured and valued than it was originally. It has a story. It's unique and beautiful because it was broken.'

A moment of silence passed between us. I leaned back, letting out a deep breath.

'No one has a future without a past. No one can become whole without being broken. In broken things, true beauty lies. Grief and loss remind us of what's important. Without darkness, light cannot exist. Think about it.'

And I did. I never stopped thinking about it.

Little by little, I clung to this notion. It became a mantra in my life. I read everything I could find on this brilliant new idea that challenged my previous way of thinking.

In a poem by Mary Oliver called 'The Uses of Sorrow' she wrote, 'Someone I loved once gave me a box full of darkness. It took me years to understand that this, too, was a gift.' It took a little time and reflection, but in hindsight, the unexpected gift brought beauty, strength, and gratitude into my life.

The pain I had lived through was not easy. And it wasn't fair. But I was not alone. My story of pain and breakdown was both unique and universal at the same time. It lit a fire within me, and I took that box of darkness and filled it with gratitude and hope.

That afternoon, under the pastel Queensland sunset, I took all the lessons and chose not to allow another minute to be stolen, emerging out the other side into the light.

It was like seeing the early signs of spring after a cold and dark winter. Trees, once bare and skeletal, begin to unfurl delicate buds, preparing to flower. Like the horizon line that was concaved and endless, I faced a world without fences.

As we packed up and drove home that night, I felt gratitude for the feeling of lightness in my soul. The sky above the windshield was clear, the stars, fire.

My grief had diminished and was replaced with boldness. I would no longer wear the shackles of a broken marriage or the traditions of my upbringing. Everything I thought I knew was laid out to be questioned. I needed to know who I was underneath it all.

Who might I have become if I had not lived within these confines? Who would I have loved? What would I have believed? How much of who I was and the life I had lived had been my idea? I was in my thirties, and while I had experienced many things, I knew so little about others, and especially about myself.

It wasn't only my husband who had held the keys to my cage; it was society, my parents, and the church. I am a wild animal, never meant for cages. They were created to protect tradition and institutions. In families, religions, and cultures, there are institutional allegiances that we are compelled to live by a skin we must fit, a flock we must follow. I took a hard look at my faith, my life, my sexuality, my friendships, my career, my life ambitions and asked myself if any of it was what I wanted. I was drawn to people who symbolised that freedom I craved.

Tereasa and Sarah had lived their lives liberated, having taken the time to explore and celebrate who they were. They had stories and experiences that I could only ever wonder about. In the following months, I let go of my inhibitions, the expectations, and the restraints.

Like a wild horse running without bounds, I was free and wildly out of control. Every belief and life choice I had was open to be renovated. I was testing my ideas, beliefs, faith, and the boundaries of my sexuality. I had time to run wild – to recreate myself, and to rebuild a life that would be built by me, for me.

I experimented to see what fit and concluded that when the chips finally fell, they fell somewhere between who I had always been and the person I thought I was. I felt greatly comforted by that. When my marriage ended, I grieved the loss of old dreams. How could I love or trust again, giving power to another to break me? I wasn't sure I would ever be ready for such vulnerability.

I tried dating again at my friend's suggestion to 'get back onto the horse'. He was a friend, a soft place to fall, listening, and teaching me about myself. I craved emotional intimacy, something I'd never had before.

I knew he was no threat, but my body was on red alert. Poised for flight, in panic mode. I wondered if it was a response to trauma, this heightened hypervigilance. I self-sabotaged every step forward, shielding my heart. His heart was maimed and broken too.

Then I read Finding Love Again by Carolyn Martinez, which was both a blessing and a curse. It became apparent as I completed self-quiz sections on the final pages, writing a list of what I wanted and valued in a partner, that the man I had been seeing wasn't him. At the time, it was an inconvenient truth and one I struggled to face. He was a safety blanket, and I didn't want to let go. We parted ways, moving forward with our lives.

I took the time to do what made me happy. The things I had loved before but had taken a back seat to grief. Reading, photography, writing, travelling, and art. I hung out with my friends and my children. We walked in parks, circling the lakes near our home.

Springtime was in full bloom. The ducks and their young glided like arrows across the lakes, and the geese took flight, their calls like laughter. Spangles of orange and brown leaves settled on the shallow surface of the water. Their crinkled, delicate edges moved across the lake like tiny boats. The chorus of birds and cicadas came alive before dawn. Their melody reminded me that life goes on.

'Oh, give it here! I want to see the man talent on the Gold Coast!' Tereasa laughed, grabbing Lyndal's phone with a mischievous sparkle in her eye and scrolling through the Tinder profiles on the screen. She and Nina had come to stay with us for a few weeks as we had counselling and legal appointments to finalise the surrogacy parenting order for Nina. Tereasa would finally be recognised as her legal mother in the eyes of the law.

The house was full of girls and mischief. Rolling my eyes, I watched as they sat on the carpet, giggling and engrossed in swiping left or right.

'How do you even do that?' I asked Lyndal, my face recoiling with disdain as I pointed at her phone.

She smirked. 'Do what?'

'That. Tinder. Aren't you afraid you'll get a disease? Have you seen the losers that are out there?' I argued, incredulous.

'Sure have…' She grinned. 'I've seen plenty.'

I groaned, shaking my head.

'I want to see what kind of guys are out there. You can sign up. You're single,' Tereasa piped up, her eyes bright as though she'd had an epiphany.

'You should go on a date,' she insisted, laughing.

'No. Not going to happen.' I shook my head.

'Oh, come on, it'll be fun. All you have to do is have dinner with five nice young men… Dinner and conversation. That's all.'

My eyes rolled. 'And you think the Gold Coast actually has five nice young men?' I threw her a dirty look. She ignored me.

'Tinder or Plenty of Fish?'

'No,' I insisted. 'I've seen the calibre of dudes on those apps. Not my scene.' I laughed, pointing to Lyndal, who had returned to flipping through the photographs on her phone again.

'Where are the good ones these days, then?' Tereasa asked no one in particular.

'Married or gay.'

'Come on!' she teased, stifling laughter, and trying to muster a serious face.

Thinking for a moment, I finally replied hesitantly.

'Maybe eHarmony? It's been a long time since I've even looked at one of those, but the ads have guys who don't look like total serial killers. That's always a plus.'

Tereasa met my eyes again in silence with a wry smile.

'Come on…' she teased. 'Five dates. Just dinner. It'll be fun.'

I met her stare with a look of defiance. 'Fine. Just dinner. But if I get any dick pics, I'm out.'

She looked amused, knowing she had won the round.

What had I got myself into? After a long relationship, I was out of touch with this dating thing. I felt old, even though I was still in my early thirties. My expectations were firmly grounded in the grim reality of online dating: 65% total creeps, 30% dull and boring, and 5% potential to want to have dinner with. These were not good betting odds.

'So, how's this going to go?' I asked. 'Hi! Let me introduce myself. I'm Mel. I have twenty-two biological children to fourteen men, many of whom are married. I've impregnated more women than you have. I have a crazy ex-husband and a complicated story. That's why I'm so messed up and broken with trust issues that fuel my utter dislike for men. The jury is still out on you, buddy. Buckle up. Oh, and don't Google me.'

Tereasa laughed as I ranted.

'They're going to run screaming. I've got more baggage than Qantas.' I shook my head. 'Pass me the laptop. I can't believe I'm doing this. . .'

The Spanish restaurant on the boulevard was lit with glowing strings of lights, its red walls painted with pop art. There were clusters of tables adorned with tealight candles and bottles of red wine. Small groups gathered and engaged, deep in conversation, others at tables for two.

In my effort not to be late, I arrived early, thankful for the opportunity to collect myself.

I was given a pep talk before being ushered out the door. Tereasa was home with the kids, and this night was all mine.

A few nights earlier, on Halloween, a group of friends went out to a party to dance the night and blow off some steam. I drew the short straw, staying home to care for five sugared-up children in princess and superhero costumes, fresh from trick or treating. After the children were finally asleep, I logged into eHarmony, bored, curious, and alone. I'd almost quit a few nights before after a string of almost amusing disasters.

There was Cory the helicopter pilot with a southern cross tattoo who communicated in chats with indecent emojis. Rookie mistake. Chris, the indignant lawyer who wasn't over his ex. Carlos, a South American fuckboy, photographed in a back cape and sword, who was sure he had mastered the art of seduction. There was Mark, the furniture importer, so impressed with himself and his money, he was certain women would be too. Finally, there was Tom, a lonely, single dad who wanted someone to love him. A quick check of social media revealed he had a wife and child, the former seemingly having no idea that her husband was on the prowl. The list of ineligible men went on, a ludicrous line of suitors, five of which I was supposed to have dinner with.

After ten days, I facetiously posted a 'crazy cat lady' image on social media, entertained and accepting of this outcome becoming more likely by the day. I was the mischievous feline, stalking its prey, tiny wild animals out at night, eyes fixed with laser-like precision, batting at the elusive creature with lightning-fast reflexes. And when I was done, I would leave the dead and battered carcass on a random doorstep. I still didn't trust men. Hypervigilant and weary, this experiment was more a diversion than a vocation.

Then, my inbox notifications flashed. After running the gauntlet of questions sent to others in the getting-to-know-you process, a man sent me a message, and we started conversing.

In his profile photo, Mal looked handsome, but not too handsome. He had a kind face and honest eyes. There was no need to hide or embellish. We talked openly about many things, both meaningless and surprising. He had a decent job, liked travelling and the outdoors, and was a reader. There were no requests for inappropriate photographs, no hints of bitterness at the last woman who did him wrong, no innuendo. Tick, tick, tick. It flowed, and after a few hours, he asked if I would have dinner with him. He seemed sincere, and I agreed.

A few evenings later, I smoothed my dress and glanced at my watch, waiting for him to arrive. It was nearly six-thirty. I caught sight of a young man walking towards the restaurant. Tall and athletic, wearing black frames, pressed pants, and a white print collared shirt that barely hid a muscular physique.

He approached, and as he met my eyes, his lit up. 'Mel?' he asked curiously.

I nodded. 'Hi.'

'It's nice to meet you,' he answered.

He gestured towards the entrance to the patio area. 'After you.'

He pulled my chair out, waiting patiently for me to take a seat before sitting opposite. I could feel my pupils widening, light pouring in. I observed him as we talked, articulate and well-spoken but not pretentious or arrogant. I was comfortable. He had a quiet way of drawing you in. His eyes lit up, searching for something, deciphering me. There was something about his essence, a purity, an intensity.

We went from dinner to walking on a nearby beach as a thunderstorm approached. The sky transformed into a canvas of shifting hues, dark clouds gathering on the horizon, heralding the storm's arrival. The air was electric with anticipation, charged with energy, with alchemy. It was magical and breathtaking but also excruciating. Standing in the sand, the first droplets of rain kissed the earth, a symphony of sensation enveloping the senses – the salty tang of the sea, the cool touch of raindrops against our skin. With flashes of lightning illuminating the sky, we ran towards the car as the sky opened. We found ourselves at a café, lost in conversation as the hours passed.

We exchanged questions. Curious, investigative, but always respectful. The more I uncovered, the better it got. It neared midnight and he had an early flight the following morning. I didn't want the night to end but also, I didn't want to move too fast. The temptation to kiss him was strong, stronger than gravity. There was something special in our connection that needed nurturing. Worth waiting for.

It was both exciting and terrifying to take the chance, to leave myself open to something new, and trust that good things would come. Everything was experienced through the filter of uncertainty, but something about this felt solid. Over the following days he was working away but we texted each other constantly and talked every night for hours. I awoke, tired and happy, wondering what to do with daylight. The hours between our conversations became vast and shapeless things. Counting down the time till we'd be together again.

While we took it slowly, there were moments where my pain crept in, desperate to self-sabotage, to pull down and put a stop to anything that risked heartbreak. Falling in love can feel like stepping into the unknown, a leap of faith into uncharted territory. I realised love actually involves quite a bit of faith. There's a lot of letting go involved. Two souls in love in an intricate dance of give and take. It demands courage, letting go of inhibitions, trusting in the unknown, and embracing the beauty and complexity of human emotions, even when the outcome is uncertain.

That summer, our lives began to intertwine. Our steps steady and considered, we introduced our children and families. My girls took to him, a steady hand that was present and emotionally available. The five of us – my daughters and his son Isaac – became a family, moving in together and beginning life on a blank canvas, hopeful of creating a masterpiece.

17

In the Australian springtime, I married Mal.

It had been two years since I first laid eyes on him outside that Spanish restaurant. We quickly connected, starting a conversation that had never stopped, a bond that grew and grew. Falling in love with Mal wasn't falling at all; I finally felt like I was home.

Our wedding day was beautiful: a simple ceremony surrounded by our loved ones on a headland by the sea. The sun sparkled on the blue-green ocean. We watched whales and their calves in the distance, migrating south, sprays of salt water and the playful thrashing of their tails as they swam.

My daughters, in flowing white dresses stitched with gemstones, had removed their shoes and played with other children nearby, blowing bubbles into the breeze. Mal reached out for my hand, our fingers intertwining. His love was deep and honest, and I didn't know if I had ever been as humbled by anything in my whole life.

We travelled through France on our honeymoon, strolling a Parisian esplanade, hand in hand, spending most of our days taking walks along the Seine, and dining at quaint restaurants. We became part of the city, getting lost in it as we got lost in each other. We wandered laneways and rows of grand apartments, watching boats glide beneath the river bridges, admiring artists painting on the riverbanks, and the statues of revolutionaries that graced the cobblestone city squares.

We ambled beneath the bare trees and the evergreens, exploring the galleries and drinking espressos at cafés, and watching the world pass by.

There was no better way to begin married life as we sat on a sandstone ledge, people watching and breathing in life around us as it passed us by. A horn band played from a café, church bells rang from afar, and pigeons scattered as children skipped on the pavement. Mal pulled me close, keeping me warm from the cold winter air. His well-built arms were noticeable beneath his leather bomber jacket. I adjusted my scarf, wrapped around the folds of my coat, which hung over my dress.

It had taken some time to choose this one as I searched several Parisian boutiques to find the right one. It was Faith's Paris dress, and I had chosen it with her in mind.

We sat, absorbing every minute, soaking up the sunshine. Although I was thousands of kilometres away from where I'd begun, I knew I was where I was meant to be. It had been a journey to get here, but one worth every moment.

Green shoots of life had emerged from the ashes after a wildfire had torn across the landscape. It had proven that the death of the old made room for new beginnings and possibilities. It had taken time and work, but as I had found peace in myself and rebuilt my self-worth, the rest of my life had begun to fall into place.

To reiterate something: this is not the story of a girl who finds her prince, falls in love again, is healed and lives happily ever after. This is the story of a woman coming home to herself.

This isn't the predictable narrative arc they taught in ninth grade English class, an exposition, rising action, climax, falling action, and resolution. It's not a tidy summary that endeavours to lay shape over my lived experience, to map out a life in a linear and flowing framework.

The biggest tragedy had not been in losing my marriage; it had been in losing me and of letting that brokenness feel irreparable. A lifetime of trauma that had finally caught up to me, even as I tried to run from myself.

When any of us experiences a breathtaking loss, the future looks like a gaping black hole. How we could ever put our broken lives back together again seems like a question with no answer. One day, it hit me: the worst things to happen to me individually were the best things to happen to my character. And ever so slowly Lucas disappeared from our lives, drifting around in the depths of withered memories until he became an event, instead of a person. My story is not about what was lost, but what was found. What matters most is that which remains. The work of healing and forgiveness – not only of others but of myself. I extended as much compassion, kindness, and grace that I would to others.

Mal once asked about my heart and healing right after we started dating. 'Have you done the work?' It was a question that demonstrated insight and understanding, and I took a moment to ask myself, had I done the self-work to heal and move forward with my life? I replied that I had and would continue to. It wasn't easy; it rarely is. But after darkness and sadness came joy. Initially in small pieces, but it came, and I looked for it everywhere.

Since meeting Mal, I have fitted a lot of living into my life.

I became a surrogate for a second and third time, giving birth to a little boy and then a little girl. Being a part of the journey of the fourteen families who have become parents through donating eggs or being a surrogate has been one of the great honours of my life. These incredible people have taught me about the beauty of persistence and faith. In giving, I became richer, and each person I gave to, in turn, has given back to me.

Life can continue to test us and build resilience. Through the pandemic that impacted the world, I was one of the hundreds of thousands of nurses across the world feeling overwhelmed, exhausted, and hopeless at times. Working in an infectious diseases ward, we saw the best and worst of humanity. After it was over, one day, fatigue set in. I could not bring myself to get up and go to work. The longer I avoided going, the harder it became to return. I knew something needed to change. I studied and went on to work in the mental health sector, supporting people recovering after experiencing a suicidal crisis or enduring such profound suffering that life no longer felt worth living. It was both an honour and a privilege to be entrusted with their stories – to be the person they allowed themselves to be vulnerable with as, together, we began to pick up the pieces of their lives.

Their breakdown, their crisis, is often evidence that something in their lives is not working. That there must be change, indicating it's time to work through trauma. Every time I hold space for someone's story, it strikes me anew. When we meet, their worlds are dark. They, like many others in society, are hurting and dying in vast numbers. Setting themselves on fire. One by one.

I sit beside my clients, other imperfect humans, listening, talking, witnessing their distress, their anxiety, and their pain. To engage with this person – their suffering and their loss – is all I can do. It can be long, and ugly, and exhausting. But we are there, listening, accompanying, advocating. Over time, I went on to work in the family and domestic violence space – in refuges and in the community – where I continued to sit with people in crisis, holding space for their stories and survival.

Being in pain isn't a form of failure; it just means you're alive. It's time we stopped casting out those among us who are hurt or frightened. Those among us who have been harmed. A wound isn't contagious, but it's slow to heal if it receives no tending.

Every teacher is human. Likewise, we are not wise oracles – we're just people trying to shepherd other people through the world. We may know the right path to take, but knowing the way and consistently walking it are two different things. Everything we learn, we learn from someone who is imperfect.

They are humanity charting courses over rough seas. When they take on water and lose their way, we are the lighthouse, guiding the way because we too have sailed these water veins and their snares. We guide them to understand that while they can't control the winds, they can adjust their sails.

This doesn't mean that we will never experience challenges again. Life does not work like that. It's more like a maths class where the puzzles and exercises grow ever more complex with our life experience. But we can always keep coming back to the fundamentals and applying them again. We must remember that we are resilient and have navigated our way through challenging times before.

Hope, bright and steadfast, is an undimmable star, a fixed point in our sky. It guides us home, orients and reorients us, over and over, toward justice, compassion, liberation, and community, as the earth beneath our feet continues to shift.

The question I keep asking myself as I write this book, the question I keep insisting upon, is this: how can this story – my experience – be useful to anyone other than me? How can I share the hard-earned lessons I've learned, transforming them into words that society can digest and grow from? I wrote a story about scars, hoping to carry a light for others. It's about writing with unflinching honesty and releasing it into the world like a helium balloon, hoping it reaches someone who finds echoes of themselves in these pages. And that will be enough to sustain the message.

To you, who have found your way to this book, enduring your private and personal griefs against the backdrop of society's sickness – our collective trauma, in a culture of misogyny, violence, shame, isolation, hurt, decay, and adversity, with the overwhelming fear that things may never get better – this book is for you.

You may be looking for an answer, you may be looking for hope, something meaningful and substantial to hold on to.

Friedrich Nietzsche wrote, "He who has a why to live for can bear almost any how." His quote sums up the profound connection between purpose and resilience. When we possess a clear and meaningful reason for existence – a "why" that drives our actions and fuels our aspirations – we can find the strength to endure life's challenges, regardless of the circumstances. This inner sense of purpose acts as a guiding light, providing solace and direction amidst the darkest of times.

Having a purpose instils a sense of meaning and significance, infusing even the most mundane or difficult tasks with a sense of importance. It grants individuals a sense of agency and control over their lives, empowering them to navigate adversity with courage and determination.

In times of hardship, knowing "why" they persist gives individuals a sense of clarity and resolve, allowing them to transcend their struggles and emerge stronger on the other side.

But the "how" is also important in this story. Pain is part of a story, and it can hurt or alter and change us in a positive way. Without failing, falling, rising and trying again, there can be no mastery.

In the end, the beauty of breaking down lies not in the pain itself but in the transformation it catalyses. It is the alchemy of suffering turned to strength, of adversity transmuted into growth. It is a reminder that within every challenge lies an opportunity, within every breakdown, the seeds of a more profound and more beautiful existence.

I feel the idea breathing and growing.

Nature, history, science, and art are full of examples of beauty coming from struggle, from death and breakdown. Life is transient, a cycle. The hatchling must break through the egg, the butterfly struggles to break the cocoon, the sunlight breaks the darkness to bring us the dawn of a new day. Pressure creates diamonds and refines gold. A mountain of autumn leaves fall before winter comes and the cycle begins again.

Nothing is permanent. Destruction is part of the life cycle and so is regeneration. No one has a future without a past. No one can become whole without being broken.

In broken things, true beauty lies in the art of all those precious scars. Grief and loss remind us of what is important. Without darkness, light cannot exist.

There are an infinite number of ways to create a masterpiece built in our obliterated places, and my story speaks to only one. I know it's almost impossible to go from a traumatic, tragic, or life-changing experience to suddenly finding a new purpose. First, there needs to be a period of processing shock and then moving through recovery, acceptance, and adapting to a new normal. I discovered the process is not linear. My story, I can now sit with it in a quiet communion and let it speak.

The beauty of broken things lies not in their flawless perfection but in their resilience, their capacity to endure change despite the scars they bear, to remind us of the inherent strength of the human spirit, and the transformative power of embracing imperfection with grace and gratitude.

We attempt to take hurt, to pick up each broken piece and renovate it into art, to find beauty in these broken things.

ACKNOWLEDGEMENTS

To write a book is to walk through shadow and sunlight, often at once. I could not have made this journey alone.

For Tereasa, Sarah, Steph, Brooke – my ride or dies, who read drafts, answered late-night messages, and held me steady when doubt crept in: you helped shape these words more than you know. To Elle, Deb, Monica, Taysa, Christina, and Michelle, for your kindness, belief, and the ways you each showed up when I needed it most – your encouragement helped carry this work to completion. To Kylie, always a rock of encouragement, solid advice, and cheeky banter, forever spurring me on. To Belinda Lopez, who offered honesty and inspiration in those early days, and to Amelia Saw, whose authenticity, wise counsel and friendship mean so much. For Rachael, Kerstin, Kristina, Cass, Rosie, Lorena, Rebeka and Tania, thank you for your support and encouragement.

To my children, who filled the spaces between paragraphs with stubborn strength, laughter, and beautiful chaos – you remind me daily why telling these stories matter.

For Charlotte, Julie, Nicole, Mel, Jaye, Trudi, Kim, Maree, Dee, and Lou – each of you has taught me something different about what it means to endure, to rebuild, and to keep believing in the goodness of life. You've shown me that resilience isn't just surviving the storm – it's learning to dance in the rain and to find beauty in the wreckage.

For Carolyn, where writing this book began and where it found its ending – your faith, patience, and gentle guidance turned scattered thoughts into something whole. And to the team at Hawkeye: thank you for seeing the heart of this work and helping it beat stronger.

To my love, Mal: thank you for being my anchor and my wings – for the quiet moments, the long conversations, and your unwavering belief that these words mattered, even on the days I wasn't so sure. To Dorothy, whose warmth, understanding, and quiet support have meant more than words can say.

And to you, the reader: thank you for turning these pages, for meeting my words with your own quiet reflection. May you find, amid these broken pieces, a small light – or at least feel a little less alone.

This book is yours now, as much as it was ever mine. *The Beauty of Broken Things* was always about more than what was lost; it is about what we choose to build from what remains.

Melissa Sharman is a writer, advocate, and domestic violence specialist whose life is a testament to resilience and transformation. Once trapped in an abusive marriage, Melissa found the courage to break free, later using her voice to help change Queensland's domestic violence laws by speaking in parliament and presenting a petition signed by nearly 100,000 Australians.

Beyond her advocacy, Melissa has given hope in one of the most personal ways imaginable – helping create twenty-three babies for fourteen families through egg donation and surrogacy. Her work as the founder of Egg Donation Australia and Australians Against Domestic Violence has provided support, education, and community to countless people navigating trauma and infertility.

Melissa's writing is shaped by lived experience, raw honesty, and unexpected humour. Featured on *The Project*, *The Today Show*, *ABC Radio National*, *Australian Women's Weekly*, and international media including *Cosmopolitan USA*, she continues to speak out for those who feel unseen.

She lives in Australia, where she works in a refuge supporting families fleeing domestic violence. *The Beauty of Broken Things* is her first book – a deeply personal memoir about turning pain into purpose, and finding beauty among the ruins.

Book reviews can make or break a book. If you liked what you read today, please do consider posting a review on Goodreads or your favourite forum.

The Beauty of Broken Things is available at hawkeyebooks.com.au and all good bookstores and libraries.

If you enjoyed *The Beauty of Broken Things*, you'll also enjoy:
Between Before and After by Edita Mujkic
Just Nat: Life in the Fast Lane with Natalie Lowndes by Natalie Kile
The Truth About My Daughter by Jo Skinner
A World of Silence by Jo Skinner
Me That You See by Anne Freeman

Praise for *THE BEAUTY OF BROKEN THINGS*

'A moving story of faith and family, of a girl growing out of trauma. Of wrong turns and sharp learning curves, of walking into beauty. Melissa Sharman is a born writer.
—*Kristina Olsson author, Boy, Lost, Shell*

'Melissa Sharman's *The Beauty of Broken Things* is not only raw and honest, but also one of the most beautiful pieces of writing I've ever read. Sharman has already touched the hearts and lives of so many, but this book will reach even further, offering readers comfort, courage, and a reminder that even in our darkest moments, there is hope.' —*Rachael Johns, author*

'Does one keep secrets or do your secrets keep you?' An exquisitely evocative, painful yet optimistic story of childhood trauma, domestic abuse and the ultimate gift of giving joy to families through egg donation and surrogacy. Bright, illuminating, vulnerable, wise, evocative, and generous.'
—*Cass Moriarty, author of Parting Words and The Promise Seed*

'Equal parts shattering and life-giving, this memoir shows how a woman can walk through fire and still cradle the world with open hands. A triumph of spirit and storytelling.'
—*Michelle Faye, author of Invisible Prison and DFV advocate*

'Raw. Unapologetic. Necessary. This is what resilience looks like when it finally speaks. A story that reminds us our darkest chapters can still write a radiant future.'
—*Renee Eaves, author of Flirt with Justice and social justice advocate*

Praise for *THE BEAUTY OF BROKEN THINGS*

'Moving, confronting and ultimately uplifting. The core of this story is female friendship. The strength of it; the sheer necessity of it; and how women, together, can rise, support, and make change. A book for anyone who has suffered at the hands of another; for those who believe in the strength of human will; and for readers who devour tales of determination, love, and friendship.
—*Lorena Otes, author of Solo Mum by Choice*

'A complex and rich narrative of one woman's survival, eclipsed only by her profound capacity to love. Her insightful prose safely guides readers through a lifetime battling abuse and control whilst she refused to yield to circumstance. Set against a backdrop of violence The Beauty of Broken Things navigates complexities of identity, faith and family, and how love can completely redefine them.' —*Taysa, The Good Feelings Desk*

'A hauntingly beautiful journey that is unique and heartrending. Melissa wields her literary skill like a surgical blade that infuses her soul onto the page.' —*Kylie Chan, author*

'Readers will first fall in love with Sharman's prose, her elegant metaphorical language expertly woven into her raw tale, and will come away with a seed of hope in their heart and the belief that there is always help out there. This book is a vivid reminder that life is precious, and I deeply commend Melissa for her bravery in sharing this story that will undoubtedly help so many others.'
—*Bex Hall, editor and reviewer*